A Capital Budget Statement

for the U.S. Government

Studies of Government Finance

TITLES PUBLISHED

A Capital Budget Statement

for the U.S. Government

MAYNARD S. COMIEZ

Studies of Government Finance

THE BROOKINGS INSTITUTION

WASHINGTON, D. C.

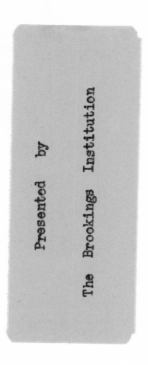

Foreword

THE GROWTH OF THE FEDERAL BUDGET in recent years has led to renewed public interest in federal budget concepts, budget accounting, and budget presentation. Because of the impact of the budget on economic activity and the political and economic importance attached to budget surpluses or deficits, politicians, scholars, and other interested groups and individuals have become increasingly aware of accounting practices. One budget and accounting concept that has aroused considerable public interest in the past and is frequently in the forefront of public discussion is the concept of a federal capital budget.

Much of what has been written on capital budgeting has concentrated on the procedures used by state and local governments and business firms. Very little empirical research has been done to determine how a capital budget might have affected the official budgetary statements of the federal government. The objective of this study is to illustrate the effect of a federal capital budget on the official figures by applying various capital budgeting concepts to the actual data for the period fiscal year 1955 through 1963.

This study was prepared by Maynard S. Comiez of the U.S. Bureau of the Budget. The assistance and comments of Samuel M. Cohn of the Bureau of the Budget were especially valuable to the author during all phases of preparing the manuscript. He is also grateful to Joseph A. Pechman, Director of Economic Studies at Brookings and Executive Director of the National Committee on Government Finance, and to Charles L. Schultze, formerly of the University of Maryland and the Brookings Institution and now Director of the Bureau of the Budget. Valuable suggestions were made by the reading committee consisting of Jesse Burkhead,

Syracuse University; Samuel B. Chase, Jr., Brookings Institution; Samuel M. Cohn, Bureau of the Budget; Gerhard Colm, National Planning Association; and Richard Goode, International Monetary Fund. Others who read all or part of the manuscript and offered helpful comments were Carl W. Tiller, Joseph E. Reeve, and William B. Ross. Peter D. Beaves, a graduate student summer intern at the U. S. Bureau of the Budget, did a large part of the early statistical work during the summer of 1962. The manuscript was edited by Charlene Semer. Harriet J. Halper and Maude A. Klock assisted in checking the statistical work. Catherine Mallardi and Allene Memmer typed the draft and final manuscript.

The author also wishes to express his appreciation to the U.S. Bureau of the Budget for granting him the time to work on this study and for making available to him earlier file materials and fragmentary studies of this subject. The author takes full responsibility for the facts and figures in this study; the views expressed are his own and do not necessarily reflect those of the Bureau of the Budget or any of its staff.

This study is part of a special program of research and education on taxation and public expenditures, supervised by the National Committee on Government Finance and financed by a special grant from the Ford Foundation. The views expressed in this study do not purport to represent the views of the National Committee on Government Finance or the Advisory Committee, or the staff members, officers, or trustees of the Brookings Institution, or the Ford Foundation.

Robert D. Calkins
President

September 1965
Washington, D. C.

Studies of Government Finance

Studies of Government Finance is a special program of research and education in taxation and government expenditures at the federal, state, and local levels. These studies are under the supervision of the National Committee on Government Finance appointed by the trustees of the Brookings Institution, and are supported by a special grant from the Ford Foundation.

MEMBERS OF THE ADVISORY COMMITTEE

Contents

Text Tables

Chart

Appendix Tables

CHAPTER I

Introduction

THE FEDERAL BUDGET serves several purposes. It is both a financial report and a plan for the future. It sets forth the President's proposed program for the government and the anticipated financial requirements for carrying out that program. It thus also represents the President's requests for legislative action, since Congress acts upon program proposals before it provides funds to carry them out. Further, the intensive review and screening process that is used to formulate the budget is an important step in the management and administration of the government's broad range of activities. Finally, the budget is an economic document, for it contains recommendations that must take into account the impact of government taxation and spending on the economic system of the United States.

The size and growth of the federal budget have aroused public interest in federal budget concepts in recent years. There has been particular interest in the surplus or deficit since these figures are commonly, and probably mistakenly, interpreted as a measure of the economic impact of federal expenditures and of the "fiscal responsibility" of an administration. Because of the effect of the federal budget on economic activity, and the political and economic importance attached to budget surpluses or deficits, politicians, scholars and other interested groups and individuals have become increasingly aware of federal accounting practices.

In recent years, several organizations have reviewed the financial statements of the federal government principally to determine what budget concept provides the most meaningful explanation of the government's fiscal and program operations. The Chamber of Commerce of the United States, at the request of President Kennedy, appointed a committee which looked into and reported on the problems of federal budget presentation, and offered suggestions for improvement.[1] In 1962, the editors of the *Review of Economics and Statistics* invited a number of distinguished experts to participate in a day-long symposium to discuss the federal budget and budgetary accounting.[2] Twelve economists contributed nine papers to this symposium, providing critical analyses of budgetary accounting practices and policies. The general conclusion was that current policies and practices were unsatisfactory. More recently, a conference sponsored jointly by the Woodrow Wilson School, Princeton University, and the Committee for Economic Development was held at Princeton, New Jersey, on October 12, 1964, to discuss the federal budgetary process and related matters, including budget concepts.

The Capital Budget Concept

One budget concept that has aroused public interest in the past, and is again in the forefront of public discussion, is the concept of a "capital budget." The present federal budget can be characterized as a unitary budget in which no accounting distinction is made between current and capital transactions. A capital budget, in essence, involves a two-way character classification of budget expenditures—capital and current. A capital budget also usually involves linking the capital account to some form of financial plan, generally, but not necessarily, loan financing.

The volume of literature devoted to an analysis and appraisal of capital budgeting is extensive.[3] Much of what has been written

---

[1] Chamber of Commerce of the United States of America, *Report of the Committee for Improving the Federal Budget* (Washington, D.C., Oct. 19, 1962).

[2] *The Review of Economics and Statistics,* Vol. 45 (May 1963), pp. 113-47.

[3] See, for example, Walter W. Heller, *An Analysis of Proposals for Capital Budgeting in the United States* (Washington: Committee for Economic Development, mimeo., 1954); Richard Goode and Eugene A. Birnbaum, "Government Capital Budgets," *International Monetary Fund Staff Papers,* Vol. 5 (February 1956), pp. 23-46; Jesse Burkhead, Chapter 8, "The Capital Budget," *Government Budget-*

recently, however, has concentrated on capital budgeting for munici-
palities and business firms. Moreover, almost without exception,[4]
the previous literature has been confined to the theoretical aspects
of the problem, and has not attempted to measure the specific impact of various proposals on the budget structure.

The present study seeks to accomplish three objectives: First,
to define the conceptual alternatives of a capital budget; second,
to summarize the major issues of capital budgeting, concentrating
on the various arguments for and against it as an appropriate and
desirable form of budgeting for the federal government; and, third,
to supplement the literature on capital budgeting with an empirical
case study designed to show what the U.S. budget would have
looked like, under various assumptions, if there had been a capital
budget during fiscal years 1955 to 1963.

The Structure of a Capital Budget

The term "capital budget" has been used rather loosely. In fact,
it has been said that "there are so many kinds and varieties of capital budgets that a general definition or a general description of procedures is impossible."[5]

The mere characterization of budgetary expenditures and receipts as current or capital in nature does not adequately define a
capital budget; this must be done in terms of its structure and its
purpose. Designing a particular budget is a process of choosing
from a set of alternative definitions and methods the combination
that will best serve the purpose at hand. How well these purposes

---

ing (John Wiley and Sons, Inc., 1956), pp. 182-211; James A. Maxwell, "The
Capital Budget," *Quarterly Journal of Economics,* Vol. 57 (May 1943), pp. 450-
65; Richard A. Musgrave, "The Nature of Budgetary Balance and the Case for
the Capital Budget," *American Economic Review,* Vol. 29 (June 1939), pp. 260-
71; Gunnar Mydral, "Fiscal Policy in the Business Cycle," *American Economic
Review,* Vol. 29, Part 2 (March 1939), pp. 183-93; United Nations, *Budgetary
Structure and Classification of Government Accounts* (1951); Beardsley Ruml,
A Budget Reform Program (The Seventh Company, Inc., 1953); John R. Hicks,
The Problem of Budgetary Reform (Oxford: Clarendon Press, 1948); Fritz
Morstein Marx, "The Divided Budget in Scandinavian Practice," *National Tax
Journal,* Vol. 8 (June 1955), pp. 186-200.

[4] The principal exception is the study by Heller, *op. cit.,* reviewing alternative
proposals and appraising the arguments for capital budgeting.

[5] Burkhead, *op. cit.,* p. 182.

are served by use of a capital budgeting technique can only be judged by comparing results of particular budgets with specified features.

A wide range of choices must be made before a particular capital budget can be shaped. Some of these choices are definitional: what is the appropriate concept of capital? Other choices involve presentation: should the budget show *gross* capital expenditures in the capital account, or should it show annual depreciation charges in the current account and *net* capital outlays —gross capital expenditures less depreciation charges—in the capital account? Finally, a capital budget poses various operational alternatives: what special rules, if any, should be applied to the financing of capital, as opposed to current, outlays?

Defining Capital Outlays

In broad terms, a capital expenditure can be defined as an outlay that produces benefits—in the case of the business firm, "profits"—in periods beyond the current accounting period. While there is general agreement on this broad definition, opinions differ when a more precise classification is necessary for accounting records. Over a period of years, the accounting and legal professions, with the sanction of the Internal Revenue Service, have built up a large body of tax and other legal principles applicable to the operations of the business firm. In spite of this body of principles, the allocation of outlays between the capital and current accounts in private business often is based upon arbitrary and, in some cases, highly subjective considerations.

There is no such body of principles for government and the principles of business accounting can not be applied to government budgeting by simple analogy. A capital budget encompassing only those federal activities that are of a business nature, that involve selling goods and services to the public, would be highly limited in scope. Only the capital purchases of such agencies as the Post Office, the Tennessee Valley Authority, and so forth would be included, while the hospital outlays of the military, the hospital construction of the Veterans Administration, the purchase of computers for the Internal Revenue Service, and similar outlays would be excluded. The question of ownership also complicates the problem of defining a federal capital outlay; should only federally-owned assets be included, or should assets financed by the government but owned by others, such as the interstate highway system, also be encompassed within the capital budget?

The classification of military assets presents a particularly difficult problem. On the one hand, certain military hard goods potentially may have useful lives of several years or more and provide services and benefits in the future. On the other hand, many of these same assets have a high rate of obsolescence.

Similar conceptual problems are encountered in the nonmilitary area. There may well be disagreement over whether to include in a capital account certain current developmental expenditures—expenditures for research, health, education and training—which are part of the government's contribution to "human" capital formation but which fail to meet a "durability" criterion.

On the one hand, these developmental expenditures may be more productive and hence, dollar for dollar, yield a higher stream of national benefits in the future than some physical assets. On the other hand, while these expenditures do contribute to the nation's productive potential and future income, they do not provide a tangible asset which, by present accounting standards, could be easily defended as an addition to the nation's total stock of wealth. Moreover, in terms of current accounting procedures, any attempt to assess an appropriate useful life for such "assets" would be arbitrary.

While the classification of certain expenditures as capital outlays is not currently acceptable by the accounting profession, government practices for classifying expenditures need not use the same criteria as those employed by the private sector. Accepted accounting procedures are not justified if they systematically distort allocation decisions. A government capital budget which fails to recognize in some manner investments that do not pass the "tangibility" test may prejudice expenditure decisions in favor of tangible investment projects, and possibly result in a misallocation of resources.

Defining Capital Receipts

The identification and segregation of capital items in a special budget separate from the current operating budget carries a strong presumption that capital outlays will be financed in some manner other than by current tax receipts. As noted previously, the most commonly discussed practice is to finance capital expenditures initially by borrowing. However, as a rule, accounting practices do not classify the borrowing as revenue, but rather as a source of funds necessary to finance the excess of expenses over receipts. Hence, borrowing can be thought of as a balancing item in the capital account.

The most common receipts allocated to capital budgets are: (1) transfers from the current budget, principally depreciation allowances on capital assets and loss allowances on loans, (2) repayment of loans, and (3) proceeds from the sales of existing government assets. In some cases, where capital investment is producing revenue from real property—as in the case of the Panama Canal, the Bonneville Power Administration and other such activities— a portion of current revenues could be assigned to a capital account. Of course, if this were done, depreciation allowances on the same items could not be charged to the current account. In some other cases, the surplus in the current account is transferred to the capital budget as a capital receipt, but like the proceeds from borrowing, this source of revenue is normally considered a means of financing a deficit in the capital account.

It has also been suggested[6] that revenues arising from certain taxes on private capital—such as death duties and capital levies— should be allocated to the federal capital account in order to assure that the nation's total capital stock is maintained. This view of capital focuses attention on the contribution of the government and its budget policy to total capital formation, public and private, in the economy. The comparable practice on the expenditure side of the capital account would be to include government outlays for capital formation regardless of whether they result in the acquisition of a public or private asset. This particular line of reasoning relies on a character rather than an ownership criterion for the basis of determining government capital receipts and expenditures.

It is by no means clear, of course, that death duties and other capital levies have a more depressing effect on private capital formation than do taxes on current income. As a general rule, there cannot be complete comparability between the capital accounts of

[6] United Nations, *Budgetary Structures, op. cit.*, pp. 23, 41.

the government and private sectors. Any particular receipt should be viewed from the standpoint of the government sector rather than from the standpoint of the government's impact on the private sector.[7] Therefore, death taxes and capital levies are not generally considered to be capital receipts.

A final point with respect to capital receipts is the proper treatment of certain receipts presently earmarked for capital investments—highway taxes, for example. There are two ways in which such receipts can be handled. The earmarked receipts from user taxes or various fees can be entered first as a current receipt and then a similar amount of current expenditures transferred to the capital account on the assumption that it reflects the rough equivalent to an allowance for depreciation of the capital asset. Alternatively, the earmarked receipts can be allocated directly to the capital account, in which case no depreciation allowances in the current account would be necessary. The latter alternative may be the simplest approach and is, in fact, the practice of many state governments.

Debt Financing of Capital Budgets

One characteristic common to all capital budgets is that some or all expenditures for capital assets are segregated and shown in a special budget separate from the general or current operating budget. This separation of accounts may also permit separate financial arrangements.

Expenditures for current goods and services represent a net decrease in government assets as cash balances are reduced without a corresponding increase in capital assets. A capital expenditure, however, does not change the net worth of the government no matter how it is financed. It may involve the exchange of one asset for another if it is financed from current tax receipts or from the proceeds of selling existing assets; or it may involve the simultaneous creation of a liability and an asset of equal value if it is financed by borrowing. This is the point of view of business accounting, and many proponents of a federal capital budget consider it equally valid for government. Proceeding from this line of reasoning, the advocates of capital budgeting often conclude that

[7] Burkhead, *op. cit.*, p. 232.

borrowing to finance capital outlays is justified whereas current expenditures should be financed from current tax revenues.

While early capital budgeting theory and much of the literature assume that capital outlays will be financed by borrowing, loan financing is not a necessary characteristic of a capital budget. As a matter of fact, one source favorable to capital budgeting takes the point of view that

... asset acquisition, taken by itself, is not an adequate justification for government borrowing, and a separation of current and capital accounts should not be undertaken for the purpose of rationalizing government debt creation. Rather, the separation of current and capital account transactions should be undertaken where it will contribute to an analysis of the economic significance of government activities. Such a classification should, however, never be taken as a fiscal policy guide, since the choice between financing from taxes or from borrowings must be based on purely economic considerations.[8]

Experience with Capital Budgeting

Although interest in a federal capital budget is relatively recent in this country—dating from the depression era—the concept is neither new nor unique. Capital budgeting is a widely used technique in business accounting and in the budgets of many state and local governments in the United States as well as the central governments of several other countries.

Business Practice

Historically, the business accounting procedure of segregating current expenses from capital outlays has been accepted as a necessary and proper practice for revealing the financial position or status of a business firm—that is, for revealing the true costs and the net income or net loss resulting from the operation of a business during a given period of time. The definition of business income or profit recognizes only the loss in value through physical wear and tear or obsolescence as a cost of the capital used in carrying on the business. Outlays for capital goods do not represent a cost to be deducted from revenues in arriving at net income. Rather,

[8] United Nations, *Budgetary Structures, op. cit.,* p. 12.

capital "expenses" are shown in the annual profit and loss statement not as a single charge to be deducted at the time the asset is purchased, but as a series of depreciation charges representing the annual loss in value of the capital assets in question. In large part, it is the adoption of this business accounting approach to recording and maintaining the federal government's budget and financial accounts which has appealed to many of the proponents of capital budgeting for the federal government.[9]

In addition to the segregation of capital outlays from current expenses, which is a feature of all business profit and loss statements, many business firms draw up a separate capital budget. Typically, such a budget will present the capital outlays which are scheduled to be made in the subsequent year (or longer period), and show the means proposed to finance these outlays. The role of capital budgeting in this objective is to help in evaluating needs for and the nature, cost, and timing of the acquisition of long-lived assets as well as methods of financing them. In this respect it is similar to the capital budget concept used by state and local governments.

State and Local Government Budgets

Unlike the federal government, some state and local governments have had several decades of experience with capital budgeting. The first governmental capital budgets developed in the United States were used by local communities. Because of the continuing conflict between expanding community needs and available resources, many local communities turned to capital programming and capital budgeting in order to help facilitate long-range physical and financial planning of various municipal public works projects.

At the state level, there is evidence of some capital programming as early as the middle and late 1920's. It was not until the 1930's, however, that interest in capital budgeting was really ignited. During this period, planning and programming of capital projects were stimulated by public works grants from the federal

[9] For a discussion of the management decision-making process for corporate capital expenditures, see Joel Dean, *Capital Budgeting* (Columbia University, Press, 1951); Harold Bierman, Jr., and Seymour Smidt, *The Capital Budgeting Decision* (The Macmillan Company, 1960); Ezra Solomon, ed., *The Management of Corporate Capital* (The Free Press, 1959).

government. The National Resources Planning Board in Washington encouraged states to establish new capital planning and programming procedures or improve existing ones.[10]

Many capital budget systems were originally adopted or integrated into the management processes of state and local communities in the United States to cope with the backlog of capital construction projects accumulated during the depression years. During the 1930's, revenues available for financing capital outlays were inadequate to meet the demand. This backlog of projects was augmented by the suspension of most state and local capital construction and deferral of a large part of maintenance and repair work during World War II. As a result, there was a revival of interest in and substantial development of state and local capital budgets during and immediately after the war.

In the first decade or so following World War II, as well as in recent years, various federal programs such as Housing and Home Finance Agency planning grants for community facilities and urban renewal projects were, and continue to be, instrumental in encouraging more and more local governments to adopt capital budgets. As of 1957, 198 of 813 cities in the United States with a (1950) population of more than 10,000 reported that they had a capital budget; as of 1963, 31 states had some form of capital budgeting.[11]

Throughout the history of state and local capital budgeting, the emphasis has been on (1) developing project programming and planning, (2) relating this to a method of financing these projects, and (3) providing for the implementation of these long-term financial and physical plans.[12] Capital budgeting, as used by state and local governments, does not include a balance sheet of assets and liabilities, nor does it normally provide an allowance for the estimated depreciation of assets. In other words, capital budgeting at the state and local level has given emphasis to budgeting from a capital planning and financing rather than from a capital accounting point of view. Thus, it is only analogous to a limited degree

---

[10] National Resources Planning Board, *Long-Range Programming of Municipal Public Works* (1941).

[11] *Municipal Yearbook: 1957* (Chicago: International City Manager's Association, 1957), pp. 276-91; A. M. Hillhouse and S. Kenneth Howard, *State Capital Budgeting* (Chicago: The Council of State Governments, 1963), p. 3.

[12] *Ibid.*, p. 1.

with capital budgeting or accounting as employed by business firms or as it has been proposed for the federal government.[13]

Experience of Other Countries

The extent to which capital budgeting has been adapted and integrated into the budgetary systems of many foreign governments in both developed and in underdeveloped countries also lends support to the proposal for a capital budget for the federal government of the United States. Such countries as Sweden, Great Britain, Canada, France, the Netherlands, Ecuador, the Union of South Africa and India all have a divided budget system of one sort or another,[14] in which certain capital or extraordinary items are segregated from other expenditures and receipts. In many cases, these items are financed by means of borrowing.

The Scandinavian countries maintain the most elaborate system of government capital budgeting. Sweden, for instance, has a complete system of capital budgeting, although it uses a narrow definition of capital that includes only revenue-producing or self-liquidating assets. The adoption of a capital budget in 1937 by Sweden was a logical outgrowth of the pioneering Swedish theory of fiscal policy which emphasized a balanced budget over the life of the business cycle rather than balancing on an annual basis. The original intention was that only the current account had to be balanced. However, in recent years, Sweden and many other countries have been turning increasingly to the realization that it is the overall budget surplus or

[13] For a description of existing or suggested capital budgeting practices for state and local governments, see Hillhouse and Howard, *op cit.;* James W. Martin, "A Framework for State Capital Budgeting," Bureau of Business Research, University of Kentucky, *Summary of 19th Annual Meetings of the National Association of State Budget Officers, August 20, 1963* (Chicago: Council of State Governments, mimeo.); National Resources Planning Board, *op. cit.;* Jesse V. Burkhead, *op. cit.,* pp. 183-94; Lennox L. Moak and Kathryn W. Killian, *A Manual of Suggested Practice for the Preparation and Adoption of Capital Programs and Capital Budgets by Local Governments* (Chicago: Municipal Finance Officers Association of the United States and Canada, 1964).

[14] For a review of the government capital budget and accounting systems of various foreign countries, see Richard Goode and Eugene A. Birnbaum, "Government Capital Budgets" (International Monetary Fund, Nov. 16, 1955), pp. 24-71. This document is the original mimeographed paper written by the authors. It includes a series of notes on foreign budgets and accounting systems, which were not included in the final article published in the February 1956 *IMF Staff Papers, op. cit.*

deficit that is relevant for economic policy purposes and not the current or capital account surplus or deficit.

Capital budgeting in the Scandinavian and certain other countries goes far beyond the capital budgeting of state and local governments in the United States. In addition to the separation of capital outlays from current expenditures, depreciation accounts are kept, permitting a proper comparison between budget surpluses and net increases or budget deficits and decreases in the value of government assets. This system recognizes the fact that if asset values are to be preserved current revenues must at least cover current expenditures, including an allowance for the depreciation of capital assets.

Capital budgeting, as used in some developing countries, is designed to facilitate the planning of programs which are particularly crucial for long-run growth and development. The definition of a government capital outlay in these development budgets is much more varied and is seldom limited exclusively to an accounting definition. Thus, the capital budget is likely to include outlays not only for physical assets but also for other development services and human resources. Such outlays are generally segregated in a separate account so that they can be given the special type of management review and analysis that they require.

Proposals for a Federal Capital Budget

During the Great Depression there was considerable debate in the United States on the desirability of instituting a double budget to accommodate extraordinary depression expenditures. In 1932, the practice of using "authority to expend from debt receipts" was adopted to finance the activities of the Reconstruction Finance Corporation. This practice came into use with the understanding that such authority would be used only to finance capital or investment-type outlays which could be expected to be repaid in cash over a period of time. During the next 14 years, this practice was extended to other agencies such as the Export-Import Bank and the Federal Housing Administration. These expenditures were not counted in the conventional budget expenditure totals until 1946.

In 1933, President Roosevelt introduced a dual type of budget separating ordinary from extraordinary expenditures. This technique was used to array the ordinary portion of expenditures against current tax receipts and to justify borrowing for the extraordinary part.[15] Several years later, the dual type of budget was again thrust to the forefront of public discussion by the position on "extraordinary expenditures" taken by President Roosevelt in his budget message for the fiscal year 1940 when he said:

The public has been showing an increased interest in the adoption by the Government of a form of budget which would conform more nearly to the practice followed in commercial business. There has been some criticism of the Government's practice of including in its budgetary expenditures, amounts disbursed for loans, or for self-liquidating projects, or for other extraordinary capital outlays which increase the wealth of the Nation.
. . . While I do not advocate that the Government capitalize all of its expenditures for physical improvements, it seems to me that such portions of the cost of public projects as are clearly self-liquidating should occupy a separate category in budgetary reporting. Our financial statements, of course, should clearly reflect, in appropriate classifications, the amount of Government outlays for physical improvements that are not self-liquidating in character. We must take into account the necessity for making such of these and other changes as will permit the presentation to the Congress and to the public of more accurate and intelligible statements of the financial operations of the Government.[16]

Despite the allocation of billions of dollars for capital-type outlays during World War II, very little was for self-liquidating projects. Perhaps because of this, or perhaps because of fears of being called fiscally irresponsible, President Roosevelt's proposal for segregating the cost of self-liquidating assets was given relatively little serious consideration. Moreover, except for a request to the Bureau of the Budget by Senator Wayne Morse for a listing of capital expenditures in the proposed budget for fiscal year

[15] J. Wilner Sundelson, "The Emergency Budget of the Federal Government," *American Economic Review*, Vol. 24 (March 1934), pp. 53-66.
[16] U.S. Bureau of the Budget, *The Budget of the United States Government for the Fiscal Year Ending June 30, 1940*, pp. IX-X.

1948,[17] and a very brief discussion in the 1949 Hoover Commission Report on Governmental Reorganization,[18] capital budgeting was relatively dormant as a public issue in the United States between 1940 and the early 1950's.

At that time, as part of a general budget reform program, Beardsley Ruml, in testifying before the House Ways and Means Committee on August 12, 1953, outlined a budgetary plan for the federal government which recommended that "truly producing assets should be capitalized, and that the benefits realized from these assets should be paid for as they are consumed."[19] Under Mr. Ruml's proposed budgetary reform, current items would be financed generally by taxation and most capital items generally by borrowing. The self-financing capital investment items would be turned over to authorities who would operate and finance them. For example, government agencies housed in government office buildings would pay rent to one of these authorities. The rental payments would be regular budget costs met from current tax receipts, and the authorities would raise funds by borrowing for the cost of constructing new office buildings.

In 1959, the capital budget issue was again raised when Senator Morse and several other members of Congress introduced identical bills "To amend the Employment Act of 1946 to establish policies with respect to productive capital investments of the Government."[20] The following year, in the 1960 Presidential campaign, the Democratic Party Platform and presidential candidate specifically stated that capital budgeting for water resource development was necessary to give an accurate picture of costs and returns. Two years later, in a statement in the Senate, on September 4,

[17] *Congressional Record,* Vol. 93, Pt. 7, 80 Cong., 1 sess. (1947), pp. 8596-602.

[18] Commission on Organization of the Executive Branch of the Government, *Budgeting and Accounting* (Government Printing Office, 1949), pp. 15-16. It should be noted that the Hoover Commission did not recommend adoption of a capital budget, but simply a separation of current from capital outlays in the federal budget. Starting with the 1951 budget, each budget document has included a special analysis making this distinction. See U.S. Bureau of The Budget, Special Analysis D, "Investment, Operating and Other Expenditures," *The Budget of the United States Government.*

[19] Ruml, *op. cit.,* p. 3.

[20] S. 1244, H.R. 5135, and H.R. 5197, 86 Cong., 1 sess. (1959). Hearings on the House bills were held on June 8, 1960 by the House Committee on Government Operations.

1962, Vice President Humphrey, then Senator, called for a reform in budget procedures, including the establishment of a capital budget.[21]

During the Joint Economic Committee hearings on the *Economic Report of the President* for 1964, Representative Henry S. Reuss raised the question asking how the 1965 federal budget would appear if private business investment accounting practices were followed.[22] In January 1965, in an interview published in a national business magazine, Senator Russell Long emphasized the need for the federal budget to separate government capital outlays from current operating expenses in order to obtain a more realistic appraisal of the budget surplus or deficit.[23]

All of the recommendations concerning a federal capital budget have not been favorable. For example, in November 1960, the Committee on Federal Budgeting and Accounting of the American Institute of Certified Public Accountants, after reviewing the matter, concluded that capital budgeting would not be appropriate for the United States government as a whole. The committee indicated, however, that capital budgeting might be useful in some individual agencies where the matching of costs and revenues may be significant.[24] The 1962 Chamber of Commerce report of the Committee For Improving the Federal Budget[25] also recommended against a federal capital budget.

It is clear from the wide variety of formulations and uses of capital budgets that it is impossible to evaluate the arguments for or against capital budgeting in the abstract. It is possible, however, to weigh the advantages and disadvantages that are associated with any particular choice of features among a host of alternatives.

[21] *Congressional Record,* Vol. 108, Pt. 14, 87 Cong., 2 sess. (1962), pp. 18642-43.

[22] *January 1964 Economic Report of the President,* Hearings before the Joint Economic Committee, Pt. I, 88 Cong., 2 sess. (1964), pp. 114-15.

[23] "Is Uncle Sam Really Running in the Red?" *Forbes,* Vol. 95 (Feb. 1, 1965), pp. 13-15.

[24] Memorandum of the ACIPA Committee on Federal Budgeting and Accounting With Regard to Capital Budgeting, November 30, 1960.

[25] U.S. Chamber of Commerce, *op. cit.*

CHAPTER II

An Appraisal of Capital Budgeting

THERE ARE SHARP DIFFERENCES of opinion about the merits of capital budgeting. Although the arguments have been covered in much of the earlier literature, any study of capital budgeting would be incomplete without a brief review of the principal advantages and disadvantages.

A More "Businesslike" Accounting Approach

Perhaps the principal factor contributing to the attractiveness of capital budgeting is its businesslike approach to federal finances. It is often claimed that by distinguishing between current expenditures and capital outlays, capital budgeting facilitates the interpretation of federal finances and the implementation of policy. Many people believe, therefore, that the principles of commercial accounting should be applied to government budgeting in order to help assure effective, efficient and economical operation of government and government financial transactions.

A particular budget concept cannot be appraised except in the context of the purpose it is designed to serve. In turn, this purpose is closely related to the objectives of the organization for which the budget statement is drawn up. The basic objective of the business firm is to maximize its net income, or profits. Capital assets are purchased precisely because they are expected to yield a flow of net income over time, and thereby contribute to the basic objective of the firm.

The profit and loss statement is designed to yield information about the magnitude of net income and about the items of revenues and expenses which enter into its calculation. Net income, in turn, may be broadly defined as the revenues which remain available for distribution after deducting all expenses, including an allowance for the loss in the value of capital—a depreciation charge—which has occurred during the accounting period. The practice of segregating capital outlays from current expenses and accruing depreciation as a current expense in the business profit and loss statement follows naturally once the purpose of the business enterprise and the definition of net income are stated.

A related aspect of commercial accounting is the concept that an increase in debt matched by an increase in assets leaves the net asset position of the firm unchanged. This notion was instrumental in the adoption of government capital budgeting in the Scandinavian countries. From the viewpoint of the business firm it has considerable importance for two reasons: (1) it provides a convenient accounting principle for debt financing of capital outlays, and (2) it implies that the ability to carry the burden of a debt is directly related to the value of its physical capital stock. In turn, the value of the firm's physical capital is of little significance except as it relates to the financial success of the business in earning a profit.

By analogy, the proponents of capital budgeting argue that there is no basic difference between private and public outlays for capital assets. In the public as well as the private sector, capital outlays give rise to the expectation of a future return. Including such outlays in government expenditures for current operations without making some provision for the assets acquired gives a false impression of government finances and impedes the effective and efficient operation of the government. The presumed comparability between public and private investment outlays also sometimes leads to the conclusion that borrowing to finance the purchase of public capital assets is justified since there is no change in the net asset position of the government.

Despite the merits of commercial accounting and capital budgeting principles for recording, classifying, and summarizing financial transactions in the private business sector, the applicability of such principles to all spheres of government is questionable.[1] In the first place, the federal government seeks, through its budgetary program, to maximize national welfare. In the pursuit of this goal the relevant revenues produced by federal capital investment are not its own receipts but the incomes and other satisfactions its citizens enjoy. As a consequence, it undertakes many expenditures of a capital nature which would not properly be an entry in the balance sheet account of the business firm. For example, it may spend money on general education. The "asset" thereby created is the increase in the stock of knowledge of the nation's citizens. The "revenues" are the long-term flow of higher incomes and higher satisfactions which accrue to a better-educated society. But the federal government neither owns the asset nor has any claim to the additional "revenues" which the asset generates.[2] Moreover, the public is not generally interested in what the government's assets are worth or how much "profit" the government has made. Instead, they are more concerned with what the government is doing to promote economic prosperity and to improve the nation's welfare.

Secondly, the goal of the business firm is to maximize its profits. The net income shown in its profit and loss statement is the result of its activities and a symbol of its success or failure. In the case of the federal government maximizing net income is irrelevant as an objective although the difference between revenues and expenditures is significant as a tool that can be manipulated to influence the level of economic activity.

In the third place, the ability of a business firm to borrow—its accessibility to a major source of funds—is directly related to its asset and earnings position and also to whether it meets the test of solvency, or financial soundness. Commercial capital accounting

[1] For a discussion of the relevance of commercial accounting principles to government operations, see *Final Report of the Committee on Government Accounts* (London: His Majesty's Stationery Office, 1950), pp. 74-76.

[2] Except quite indirectly, as a fraction of the additional national income flows back to the government in the form of higher tax collections.

techniques are designed to illuminate these relationships. The real backing for the federal debt, however, is not the value of the assets which the government owns but rather its ability to collect taxes and if necessary to create money and command resources with the funds so created. The value of federal assets bears no direct relation to either of these financial powers.

A fourth reason why commercial accounting and capital budgeting principles are generally impracticable for the public sector is the difficulty of defining a capital asset and of estimating the value of existing assets. Even if acceptable principles of classification could be developed, the market value of existing capital assets must be determined before a federal balance sheet can be compiled or depreciation allowances can be computed unless it is decided to ignore the stock of government assets existing at the time a capital budget is adopted. Several methods can be used to estimate the market value of existing federal assets, but each have their limitations and no one method can be easily and satisfactorily applied to all assets.

Finally, taking a concept of financial soundness for the private business world and applying it with equal authority to the federal government is a step backward in the effort to promote a better understanding of the inherent differences between the two sectors. The reponsibility and the capacity of the federal government to foster economic growth and stability is both inappropriate and impossible for the private sector. An evaluation of capital budgeting as it might apply to the federal government cannot be made through analogy with business accounting. Rather the evaluation must be conducted in the light of how a capital budget would serve the objectives of the federal government.

Administrative Management and Control

The federal government purchases capital assets for two basic purposes. Assets may be purchased for their direct contribution to a specific national goal. For example, a flood control dam, a highway, an intercontinental ballistics missile, or a loan to a small business firm are programmatic ends in themselves. In other cases, capital goods may be purchased as an intermediate input into a federal program whose purposes are quite distinct from the nature of the asset itself—the purchase of automated equipment to reduce the costs of disbursing federal checks, the replacement of old with new trucks in the Post Office, or the construction of a new building for the Patent Office are examples of this second type. In the first case the decision to buy the asset reflects a decision to initiate, or increase the size of, a particular government program, and must be weighed against the benefits from using the funds in other federal programs. In the second case the decision to purchase the asset does not involve a choice of program but rather relates to minimizing costs or increasing the effectiveness of a program already determined.

There are advantages claimed for segregating capital from current expenditures of both types, and treating capital expenses on an accrued, or depreciation basis. An accurate statement of program costs and resource use is necessary to minimize the costs of achieving given program objectives. The accrual of capital costs in the form of depreciation charges contributes to a more accurate statement of costs and might well promote efficiency in government operations. Decisions to substitute capital for manpower, for example, may often lead to lower real costs in the long run. But if agency budgets are charged with large lump sum expenditures in the year during which the capital is purchased, this may discourage the adoption of those lower cost methods which require high initial outlays.

Reliable statements of costs, including the cost of maintenance and the alternative cost of replacement, might also be helpful for encouraging greater attention in government to the maintenance of federal property and improved property management. It would be particularly helpful for deciding whether to replace old assets, purchase new assets, or whether to rent or buy a particular asset. Recognition of the cost of maintenance and consideration of obsolescence are essential elements in deciding between maintaining, replacing or selling an asset.

Capital budgeting and accrual accounting also provide cost data helpful in deciding alternative uses for nonspecialized capital equipment that can be diverted from one use to another.[3] Such management decisions require a complete knowledge and consideration of the basic factors that determine operating costs, of which annual depreciation accruals are one of the most important.

[3] Richard Goode and Eugene A. Birnbaum, "Government Capital Budgets," *International Monetary Fund Staff Papers,* Vol. 5 (February 1956), p. 8.

It is questionable, however, whether a capital budget is needed for the purpose of effective and efficient property management. "The interests of improved property management can be at least partially served . . . by an inventory of assets . . . and other techniques . . . independent of a capital budget."[4]

Capital budgeting is also not the only means to obtain the type and variety of cost data and related information (e.g., the costs of performance) which are important for optimum decision making at the policy and management levels. A cost-based budget system of accounting for individual projects and activities satisfies the need for such information without separate treatment and financing of capital outlays in the national budget. The cost-based budget system of accounting distinguishes at the project level between expenditures for current operations and outlays for the acquisition of capital assets, and thereby permits a review of funding plans in terms of (1) those purposes yielding benefits in the immediate future (of, say, less than a year) and (2) those assets yielding benefits of greater duration (one year or more).

As a matter of record, a 1956 amendment to the Budget and Accounting Procedures Act of 1950 specifically requires accrual accounting with a view to facilitating the preparation of cost-based budgets.[5] Properly applied and appropriately supplemented by procedures designed for fund control purposes, this accounting procedure could produce reliable information on costs, income, assets and liabilities of government programs and activities.[6]

Improved Public Understanding

An important objective of government budgeting is to provide a channel of communication for keeping the general public informed and for promoting a better public understanding of govern-

---

[4] Jesse Burkhead, "The Capital Budget," *Government Budgeting* (John Wiley & Sons, Inc., 1956), p. 209. An annual inventory of federal assets is now compiled and could be useful for this purpose. See Chapter 5, pp. 64-66, for a discussion of this inventory and its limitations.

[5] Nearly 70 percent of all budget appropriation *accounts* are now kept on an accrual basis. However, most of these do not include depreciation as a cost. Moreover, the Department of Defense (military), NASA and the Department of State are the major agencies which have not yet converted to accrual accounting and these comprise more than 55 percent of total budget *dollars*.

[6] U.S. General Accounting Office, *Accounting Procedures for Federal Agencies* (1962), pp. 2-3.

mental activities and operations. A capital budget for the federal government might contribute to this objective.

Capital budgeting could provide a systematic means of gathering and presenting information on the role of the federal government in capital formation and wealth creation.[7] Our system of social accounts is incomplete without a reliable estimate of the government's contribution to the nation's wealth and the stock of capital assets which are the foundation of the means to produce present and future benefits. Such information helps to provide a more complete understanding and analysis of the behavior of the economy. It might also increase the political acceptability of federal capital outlays by assuring the voter that he is getting a productive asset in return for his tax dollar. This is of particular concern to those who believe that there is a need for increased public investment expenditures.

A capital budget might also contribute to international budgetary understanding. It might be desirable to compile U.S. budget data on a basis comparable with the data of other countries because of the continuing interest in comparing the U.S. budget surplus or deficit with the budget surplus or deficit of others. In several cases, this would require preparing a capital budget, of one form or another, for the United States.

It is generally recognized that a separation of current expenditures from capital outlays provides information which is helpful for promoting greater public understanding of government financial transactions and that it also facilitates economic analysis. It is questionable, however, whether it is necessary to have a capital budget in order to obtain the type of information that is desirable. As noted in the Goode and Birnbaum study of capital budgeting:

A formal capital budget . . . is not indispensable to the preparation of complete social accounts. Estimates of government capital formation can often be made on the basis of collateral data. The budget and public accounts, moreover, are drawn up primarily to facilitate govern-

---

[7] For a discussion of the uses of federal government wealth estimates and the problems connected with the improvement of basic data, see *Measuring the Nation's Wealth,* materials developed by the Wealth Inventory Planning Study of the George Washington University and presented by the Conference on Research in Income and Wealth to the Subcommittee on Economic Statistics of the Joint Economic Committee, 88 Cong., 2 sess. (1964), pp. 383-422.

ment management and policy making. Considerations of statistical convenience are secondary in importance.[8]

Moreover, Special Analysis D[9] in the U.S. budget already provides information on gross additions to federal assets and the government's contribution to the nation's economic wealth. This special analysis also shows the government's investment in other than physical assets—that is, federal expenditures for education, training, research and health. Admittedly, Special Analysis D does not provide information on net capital formation since it does not include an allowance for depreciation and other related charges, but such information can be obtained within a unitary budget. Moreover, further estimates of additions to capital formation and national wealth by the federal government can be derived statistically without adopting a capital budget system.

Loan Financing of Capital Assets

Many proponents of the capital budget believe that it would be a means of taking capital expenditures out from under the constraint of the "balanced budget" doctrine. Budgets have not been balanced often in recent years. However, the pressure for a balanced budget on the part of many individuals and groups has, in the view of these proponents, kept public expenditures below a desirable level. The magnitude and composition of government spending have been heavily influenced, though not completely determined, by the level of current tax receipts. According to some proponents of a capital budget, this imposes an illogical and unwise barrier to the expansion of federal capital outlays. This could be lifted by separating current expenditures from capital outlays and financing the latter by borrowing. Since the liabilities incurred by an increase in public debt would be offset by the assets acquired, the loan financing probably would not be viewed as contributing to a budget deficit.

Much of the discussion of capital budgeting from an economic point of view has centered on its utility as a means of regulating

[8] Goode and Birnbaum, *op. cit.*, p. 31.
[9] U.S. Bureau of the Budget, "Investment, Operating and Other Expenditures," *The Budget of the United States Government.*

government borrowing. Many capital budgets are characterized by a separation of financing methods as well as accounts so that capital assets are financed in whole or in part by government borrowing and current expenditures are financed by current tax receipts.

Economic Advantages

Capital budgeting is alleged to offer several economic advantages by providing the format for a workable rule for regulating government borrowing. First, it would insulate the tax system from the effect of a fluctuating volume of capital outlays. If capital outlays were financed by borrowing and current expenditures by taxation, the unstable capital component would be removed from the current budget and replaced by an annual allowance for depreciation and related charges. Current account expenditures would then be smoothed out and the need to vary tax rates would be avoided.

As shown by the empirical results in later chapters of this book, however, shifting from the present administrative budget to a capital budget does not smooth out the pattern of annual current account expenditures or, consequently, annual tax requirements. It helps some, but there are large sources of apparently erratic changes other than capital outlays. This, of course, is not too surprising since total government expenditures have increased significantly, but not always smoothly, during the period covered in this study while federal outlays for capital assets have fluctuated widely around a relatively constant level.

If the data are plotted on a semi-logarithmic scale, it does become apparent, however, that the annual deviations of current account expenditures (including an allowance for depreciation) from a steady trend are slightly less than the deviations of total administrative budget outlays. Smoothing out the rate of growth in current expenditures might minimize the need to vary tax rates in order to balance the current account. No accounting change, however, will itself modify the real economic impact of the federal government's expenditures on the economy. It is, therefore, highly questionable whether the increased accounting "smoothness" of current expenditures would warrant any changes in tax policy which would not have been desirable otherwise.

Second, capital budgeting with loan financing may provide a better allocation of the costs of public facilities between present and future generations of beneficiaries and taxpayers than does financing such outlays through current tax receipts. Since many of the facilities provided by government will be used by and benefit several generations of taxpayers, loan financing combined with a capital account which includes an allowance for depreciation distributes the cost of these facilities over time on a pay-as-you-use basis. By charging fees or levying taxes to recover the full capital cost over a period of years, all users, both present and future, pay for the benefits they receive from government capital outlays. Under our current budgetary system, where budget expenditures are financed generally through current tax revenues, the total cost of capital facilities is written off when the disbursements are made.

Of course, this should not be interpreted as implying that the real cost of government expenditures can be passed on to future generations by means of borrowing. The real cost of capital outlays is incurred when resources are used up and alternative opportunities are foregone. Even though future beneficiaries may be charged fees or taxes to help recover the financial cost of capital outlays, such charges only reflect intrageneration transfer payments which are not a burden to the generation as a whole.[10] At the time the capital outlay is made, financial resources are provided by those who purchase the government securities floated to cover the capital outlay. The capital asset yields annual benefits roughly measured by the sum of depreciation charges and interest. Since these appear in the current account budget, they will be covered by taxes or specific user charges, so that the beneficiaries (taxpayers at large or specific users) pay for the benefits as they are received, and the security holders are able to recover their initial investment plus interest.

Third, loan financing of federal capital outlays, coupled with appropriate rules for deciding which federal investments to undertake, would tend to adjust total public and private investment more closely to the volume of savings which the nation was willing to provide voluntarily, through the free market. If only those federal

[10] Unless, of course, the public debt is externally held, in which case the taxes or fees collected from the nationals of one country would be paid to the nationals of another country, resulting in a burden on the former. See A. C. Pigou, *A Study in Public Finance,* 3rd ed., (London: MacMillan & Co., Ltd., 1949), pp. 37-38. For a review of the debate on the possibility of passing on the burden of the public debt to future generations see Carl S. Shoup, "Debt Financing and Future Generations," *Economic Journal,* Vol. 72 (December 1962), pp. 887-98. The introductory footnotes to this article also present a good bibliography of the current literature on the subject.

investment outlays were undertaken which promised to yield a return (not necessarily a monetary return) equal to or greater than the interest rate on federal securities,[11] then federal capital outlays would compete for savings on an equal footing with private and state and local projects. An increased volume of federal investments, other things being equal, would tend to raise the interest rate. Some private or state and local investments would be displaced, and some additional funds would be forthcoming, either from additional private saving or from a reduction in "idle" cash balances. The total volume of investment would rise, but by less than the additional amount of government investment. How much the additional federal investment would represent a rise in total investment, how much a decrease in consumption, and how much it would reflect a displacement of nonfederal investment would depend on a number of factors, including the interest elasticities of saving, the demand for cash, and the degree of full employment in the economy.

If the public investment were tax financed, its impact on private investment and consumption would depend upon the nature of the taxes levied. Excise taxes or taxes on lower income groups would tend to reduce consumption outlays. Taxes on corporate profits or on upper income groups would tend to have a larger impact on private investment. According to some proponents of the capital budget, debt financing, combined with appropriate investment decision rules, is preferable to tax financing, since in the former case the private market would be able to decide the overall division of national output between investment (public and private) and current consumption. In the case of tax-financed federal outlays, the overall investment-consumption decision would depend upon the choice of the kind of taxes levied.

Economic Disadvantages

In opposition to the contention that capital budgeting provides a workable rule for regulating government borrowing, the following criticisms can be made:

[11] More precisely, the return from the project should be compared with the rate on federal securities adjusted upward to reflect the riskiness of the project involved. Even this is an oversimplification, but sufficiently accurate for the present discussion.

First, to the extent the rule implies that capital outlays should be covered by borrowing and current expenditures covered by taxation, it is far too rigid from the standpoint of countercyclical fiscal policy. It is generally agreed, for example, that planned cyclical variation of government expenditures, including outlays for capital projects, can provide an economic stimulus when needed. However, in many cases it is neither feasible nor desirable to exercise cyclical control over the level of capital expenditures and hence over loan financing. For many capital projects there is a considerable time lag between the project planning stage and the stage when contracts are let, obligations incurred and checks disbursed. As a result, the effectiveness of federal capital expenditures as a countercyclical force may be greatly diminished. Furthermore, there are many cases where the need for a particular capital project is unrelated to the business cycle and the decision whether to undertake the project should be made on the basis of welfare rather than fiscal policy considerations.

As long as new capital outlays exceed depreciation, that is, as long as there are continuing net capital outlays, borrowing to finance them would yield a long-run inflationary bias. While this bias has a favorable (expansionary) impact when the economy is depressed or lagging, loan financing of capital outlays during the latter stages of the business cycle would "serve to perpetuate government contributions to inflationary pressure when economic stabilization requires substantial aggregate surpluses."[12] Moreover, since all expenditures —current and capital—have an economic impact, current revenues in a boom period should be more than enough to cover just current expenditures if the government is to avoid contributing to inflation.

Of course, a divided budget with loan financing of new capital projects may not always be expansionary. If allowances for depreciation and related charges catch up to or exceed the amount of new capital outlays, the effect is just the opposite. While this would be helpful for implementing an effective economic stabilization policy during periods of inflationary pressure, a surplus of currently-financed depreciation allowances over new loan-financed capital outlays during periods of depressed or lagging economic activity would reinforce the deflationary tendency in the economy.

[12] Burkhead, *op. cit.*, p. 208.

There is no reason to believe that the amount of loan financing desirable for compensatory fiscal policy purposes will be equal to the amount of government capital outlays. While loan financing under conditions of inadequate aggregate demand may help lessen the damage to the government's economic stabilization program, decisions to finance government expenditures either by borrowing or by taxation should not be made on the basis of the current or capital character of these outlays. Rather, these decisions should be based on economic stabilization objectives related to the level of the nation's current and prospective income, production and employment.

Second, since fixed rules with respect to the loan financing of capital outlays reduce the countercyclical flexibility of the budget, their adoption would place a greater burden on monetary policy to offset inflationary and deflationary pressures. But, monetary policy itself is often under considerable pressure to help counteract other problems, such as the balance of payments. As a consequence, the combined flexibility of fiscal and monetary policy in pursuing several different objectives would be significantly reduced. In general, "the introduction of loan-financed capital budgeting would add little in the way of new weapons to [our monetary-debt] arsenal or new strength to the weapons already in it."[13]

Third, although capital budgeting with loan financing may provide a better allocation of capital costs between present and future generations, the same may not hold true as between users and non-users of public facilities.

It is difficult to predict the impact of a capital budget on the substitution of user fees for taxes. On the one hand, to the extent that loan financing of capital outlays makes it easier to secure inclusion of a particular project in the budget, the adoption of a capital budget might make it more difficult to impose user fees in cases where they are warranted. At the present time, given relatively tight budget constraints, an interest group can sometimes be induced to support legislation imposing modest user fees as the only means of securing congressional or executive approval of capital outlays from which the particular group stands to gain sub-

---

[13] Walter W. Heller, *An Analysis of Proposals for Capital Budgeting in the United States* (Washington: Committee for Economic Development, mimeo., 1954), p. 51.

stantially. Were the budget constraints on capital outlays to be loosened significantly, through the device of a debt-financed capital rule, it might be more difficult to secure passage of user-charge legislation, since the groups involved would have a greater chance of securing the desired capital outlays without agreeing to user fees.

On the other hand, the adoption of a capital budget might well be accompanied by the proliferation of self-financed projects administered by authorities authorized to issue debt, operate "businesslike" ventures, and charge fees sufficient to cover all or part of their costs.[14] Were this to occur, the market place would play a greater role in allocating resources on the basis of a pricing mechanism, in place of an allocation by governmental decision, based on a calculation of total social costs and benefits. In some cases this development could have an unfortunate effect, particularly in the distribution of benefits to needy or underprivileged groups or in the underallocation of resources to areas in which free market prices substantially understate total social benefits. This need not happen, of course, since appropriate subsidies could be paid out of the current account budget, if necessary, to accomplish desired social goals. Nevertheless, if loan financing of capital outlays encouraged too great a reliance on self-financed and self-liquidating projects, the result might be an excessive use of fees instead of general taxes as a means of covering the annual costs of public services.

Fourth, debt financing of the capital portion of a capital budget might result in a distortion of spending decisions and a misallocation of resources. An unjustifiable amount of resources might be allocated to the capital account at the expense of the current account or of the private sector if debt financing of federal capital expenditures made these outlays appear more desirable or easier to undertake. Since many federal investments in "human capital" (education, health, training, and so on) would probably not qualify for inclusion in a capital budget, investment in physical capital could easily be overemphasized in relationship to human capital. On the other side of the coin, since the definition of a capital asset must be arbitrary, particularly in the case of the federal govern-

---

[14] A number of proposals for a federal capital budget (for example, the Ruml proposal) and the experience in foreign countries call for authorities to construct, own, operate, and finance government projects of a self-liquidating character.

ment, budget officials and legislators may find it tempting to characterize unwarrantedly many expenditures as "capital outlays" in order to avoid the requirement of financing such expenditures out of current tax receipts.

Conclusion

The case for a federal capital budget involving separate loan financing for capital outlays, is not persuasive. Proper classification of government receipts and expenditures is a fundamental requisite of a budget system useful to policymakers and the public alike. The distinction between current and capital outlays for the federal government is obviously a move toward identifying pertinent categories, and can be used for such purposes as analyzing the economic impact of government capital formation on the private sector, and helping to estimate the federal component of national wealth. However, capital budgeting is not required in order to obtain the expenditure character classification necessary for economic analysis. Present statistical estimating techniques using data already available in the budget document and supplemented, if necessary, by additional data from department and agency accounting records provide as much information as could be generated by a formal capital budget and as much precision as economic analysis requires.

A distinction between current and capital transactions with appropriate annual allowances for depreciation and probable losses on loans could contribute to a measurement of the flow of government services, cost trends of government activities, and the cost portion of the benefit-cost relationships between competing government programs. It would facilitate the planning and operation of those activities which are concerned with the management of government assets as compared with activities which are concerned primarily with the disbursement of funds.

Here again, however, it is not necessary to have a federal capital budget in order to provide the cost and other accounting support necessary for effective, efficient and economic measurement and control of the assets under the jurisdiction of the government. Business-type budgets and accounting are already required of all government corporations specifically covered by the Government

Corporation Control Act, and for some government activities that operate as revolving funds. All Departments and agencies have been directed to move toward adopting accrual accounting and cost-based budgeting and the use of these methods may increase in future years. Cost accounting can be accomplished within the present federal budgetary system and can provide information on work done at every stage with reference to the resources used and the costs incurred in doing it.

Finally, the budgetary process should be used to help plan and implement the government's economic program. However, capital budgeting is not an appropriate tool for planning or implementing fiscal policy. Capital budgeting cannot and should not be used as a guide for deciding whether sound fiscal policy requires a change in the level of government expenditures or whether there should be more or less capital rather than noncapital expenditures. Nor should it be used to determine whether the budget should be balanced or unbalanced or whether federal expenditures should be financed by means of current tax receipts or by borrowing. Decisions with respect to these matters should be made in the light of economic and monetary considerations. Such decisions are best formulated within a budgetary framework such as the federal sector of the national income accounts or the consolidated cash statement.

CHAPTER III

Summary of the
Empirical Study

A MAJOR SHORTCOMING of the previous literature on capital budgeting is that it lacks an analysis of how capital budgeting would actually affect the federal budget. The remainder of this book is intended to fill this gap. It presents the results of an empirical study that was undertaken to show what the federal budget for the fiscal years 1955 to 1963 would have looked like if the United States had practiced capital budgeting during this period.

At the outset, it should be stated explicitly that the results obtained from this study are based on events that are after the fact. Conceivably, if the United States had practiced capital budget accounting during the period studied, a number of different decisions might have been made with regard to alternative or additional programs.[1] However, this study is not concerned with what might have happened. Rather, its only concern is to discuss and analyze the results obtained by converting the federal budget to a form of capital budget.

[1] See Aaron B. Wildavsky, "Political Implications of Budgetary Reform," *Public Administration Review*, Vol. 21 (Autumn 1961), pp. 183-90, where the author argues that the likelihood of budget reform is inevitably based on making changes in the "who gets what" of government decisions.

Budget Data Used

The administrative budget of the United States is the conventional statement of the receipts and expenditures of the federal government. Unlike the consolidated cash budget which includes all the government's receipts from and payments to the public, the administrative budget covers only the so-called "federally-owned" funds of the government, or those funds which belong to the federal government *per se* rather than to certain, identifiable groups —however large—such as investors in the social security trust funds. The administrative budget identifies the total receipts and expenditures of federally-owned funds. The administrative budget surplus or deficit represents the difference between total budget receipts and total budget expenditures.

Ownership of assets is a convention of the generally understood concepts of capital accounting. Since the administrative budget of the federal government represents transactions of "owned" funds, it seems to be the logical starting point for dividing transactions by their capital or current nature. Therefore, the first part of this empirical study concerns itself with the administrative budget.

The receipts and expenditures of trust and deposit funds and the net financial transactions of government-sponsored enterprises are not included in the administrative budget. It therefore excludes the capital expeditures of the highway trust fund, the secondary market operations of the Federal National Mortgage Association and the Veterans Administration life insurance loan programs. The expenditures of these programs are not reflected in the administrative budget data on which most of the capital budget models analyzed and discussed in this study are based. The consolidated cash budget, developed some years ago, includes all the government's transactions with the public, including the trust funds, deposit funds, and government-sponsored enterprises.

One significant purpose and merit of current-capital accounting could be to measure the allocation of costs and benefits over time. By dividing the administrative budget into separate current and capital accounts, it is possible to obtain a better understanding of the time phasing of government costs, that is, of the resources applied to government programs. However, there is a definite limitation to the significance of the figures used in this study because the administrative budget is not on an accrual accounting basis although detailed cost figures are available for many federal activities.

In general, the administrative budget records expenditures at the time government disbursing officers issue checks. Receipts are recorded partly on a collections basis (as the cash is received and placed under accounting control) and partly on the basis of confirmed deposits (as deposits are acknowledged by the depository banks). This essentially cash basis of accounting may be helpful for other purposes, but it should not be used to measure or allocate costs. What is needed for cost measurement purposes is the dollar value of goods and services consumed during the accounting period. This kind of measure is derived from a system of accounts which shows expenses actually accruing during a given period. Such an accrual basis for keeping accounts separates expenses actually occurring, for goods used or services being rendered, during the accounting period from funds for expenses of prior or subsequent periods.

Capital Budget Variants

There are many capital budget models that can be set up and analyzed, all with some reasonably defensible basis or rationale. Some of these models might involve variations in the definition of a capital asset. Other capital budget models could be set up to reflect differences in rates of depreciation, in loss rates on loans, or straight line versus accelerated depreciation accounting. There might also be alternative models to deal with the question of whether an allowance for depreciation should be made only for assets acquired after the establishment of a capital budget or whether depreciation allowances should be taken on all assets including those acquired prior to the establishment of a capital budget.

With so many variations possible, it is only reasonable to ask: Assuming that a capital budget is proposed, which capital budget statement is most suitable for the federal government?

In order to evaluate the results obtained from the models examined in this study, it is necessary to discuss briefly those issues that have a direct bearing on whether a particular capital budget model is a realistic choice for the federal government. The issues involved are basically five in number:

1. Should an allowance be made for depreciation and related charges?

2. If a depreciation allowance is made, should it cover assets acquired prior to the establishment of the capital account?

3. Should the concept of capital be limited to assets owned by the federal government or should it be broadened to also include assets that are federally financed but not federally owned?

4. Should the capital budget include only those funds encompassed by the administrative budget, or should it include all cash receipts and payments of the federal government as in the consolidated cash budget?

5. Should the concept of capital include or exclude military assets?

Many of these issues involve the question of whether government budgeting need necessarily be "businesslike." Many proponents of a federal capital budget advocate it because they would like to see the government's budget presented in a more "business-like" fashion. Moreover, in some cases, only the adoption of certain business accounting criteria makes it possible to construct a federal capital budget in which the definition of federal capital is held within reasonable bounds. Nevertheless, as pointed out in Chapter II, the purposes of the federal government and business firms are quite different. Hence, the mere fact that it is necessary to apply certain business accounting practices in an empirical study of government capital budgeting should not itself be taken as an argument that such budgets are more "businesslike" than, and therefore preferable to, current federal accounting procedures.

Depreciation Allowances

Proper capital budget accounting practices should include an allowance for the wear and tear and obsolescence of the government's physical assets and for the probable loss on financial assets. Both accrual and cost accounting explicitly recognize this requirement. Failure to consider all such costs would understate the total cost of providing government services, and critically limit the usefulness of such cost data for determining and appraising cost trends and benefit-cost relationships. It would also limit the validity of comparing budget surpluses and net increases or deficits and decreases in government assets. Finally, without an allowance for depreciation and related charges, no provision is made for replacing assets when they wear out or for retiring the public debt issued when capital assets are acquired.

Depreciation of Prior Assets

A case can be made for either including or excluding assets from the depreciable property base according to whether they were acquired prior to the time when a federal capital budget is established. Exclusion of previously-acquired assets might be justified because there would have been no capital account prior to adopting a capital budget so that expenditures for capital outlays would have been written off—fully depreciated—in the same year in which the outlays were made. Therefore, at the time that initial separation of current and capital expenditures is undertaken, it should not be necessary to make any provision for depreciation allowances for assets acquired in the past.

Excluding prior assets is also valid if capital budgeting is adopted in order to provide a workable rule for government borrowing. Since the use of borrowing in the past was not limited solely to the purchase of physical or financial assets, it is not possible to relate the previous increase in debt with an increase in assets. Therefore, if a capital budget were adopted, it would not be necessary to make an allowance for depreciation on existing assets since such allowances would be unrelated to the retirement of outstanding public debt.[2]

On the other hand, if a net increase in government assets corresponds with a net increase in government debt, it is necessary to consider all previously-acquired assets even though they have already been written off. Assets acquired before the institution of a capital budget should be considered if capital budgeting is to be useful for estimating the government's net contribution to capital formation or to the nation's wealth. Gross capital acquisitions must be adjusted by the amount of real depreciation and loss al-

---

[2] Gerhard Colm, *The Federal Budget and the National Economy* (Washington: National Planning Association, 1955), p. 97.

lowances for assets acquired previously even though they have been fully depreciated for accounting purposes in earlier budgets.[3]

The inclusion of prior assets is also necessary if capital budgeting is to help determine and appraise cost trends in order to improve the efficiency of program inputs. It is essential for this purpose to account for the costs of all factor inputs. Even though an asset may have been acquired prior to the existence of the capital account, its purchase price represents a cost to the government of providing certain goods and services over a period of time. To exclude these assets from the property base for depreciation purposes would understate the total cost of current government operations.

Since the most practical use of a federal capital budget would be to help provide accurate cost data and reliable information on the government's contribution to net capital formation, it is concluded that assets acquired prior to the establishment of a capital account should be included in the government's property base for depreciation purposes.

The Inclusion of Assets Not Federally Owned

It is a well-established principle in private accounting that ownership is an essential requirement for capital and depreciation accounting. Implicit in the concept of ownership is the control over the use of capital assets during the period when they will be providing benefits and services and the disposal of these assets.

One particular problem that arises under a criterion of capital that includes federally-financed, as distinguished from federally-owned, assets is whether it would be necessary or even proper for the federal government to include in its current account an allowance for depreciation on assets such as schools, hospitals, and conservation projects that it does not own, operate, or pay to maintain. This problem involves in part the balance sheet treatment of federal assets and liabilities. Is it proper, for example, for the federal government to show on its balance sheet those assets that do not belong to the government? If these assets do not appear on the balance sheet, then loan financing of nonfederally-owned capital

[3] *Ibid.,* p. 97.

assets would contradict the view that an increase in federal debt does not change the net worth of the government as long as the debt is offset by a comparable increase in capital assets.

There is no simple answer to the question of whether to include only federally-owned or all federally-financed capital assets. On the one hand, there is the precedent of existing business accounting practice which, if accepted, would lead to the conclusion that only federally-owned assets should be charged to the capital account. On the other hand, it can be argued that the objectives of the federal government are not the same as those of a business firm and, therefore, the government is not committed to following business accounting practices. If federal expenditures for additions to state, local and private assets are excluded from the capital account this would grossly understate the government's contribution to capital formation and the capacity of the nation to produce a greater national income in future years. For this reason, therefore, it might make sense to broaden the scope of the capital account to include federal expenditures for nonfederally-owned assets.

A federally-owned capital concept has been used to classify expenditures in most of the budget models in this study. However, in order to provide a comparison with capital budgets that define capital to include all federally-financed assets, three of the models in this study have been adjusted to incorporate federal expenditures for additions to state, local and private assets in the capital account.[4] A fourth model, Case VI, based on the consolidated cash statement, starts with the assumption that all federally-financed assets will be included in the capital account.

Consolidated Cash Versus Administrative Budget

There are two major differences between the administrative budget and the consolidated cash budget: (1) the cash concept is more comprehensive and complete than the administrative budget because it includes the receipts and expenditures of trust funds and government-sponsored enterprises as well as funds wholly owned by the federal government; and (2) the cash concept excludes intra-governmental transactions, that is, transactions between budget and trust fund accounts.

[4] These adjustments are made for Case II, Case V, and Case VII and are shown in Appendix F.

There is not complete agreement that all of the trust funds and their transactions should be included in the consolidated cash budget. The treatment of government-sponsored enterprises is particularly controversial. The issue involved is whether these funds and their transactions are properly classified as federal government activities. It seems apparent, however, that the federal government has a substantial equity interest in or moral responsibility for the financial soundness of each of the trust funds. It seems consistent and proper, therefore, to classify these funds as a part of the federal government, and to include their related financial transactions in a federal capital budget.

One point mentioned earlier bears repeating at this time. Both the consolidated cash and the administrative budget concepts are based on cash money flows. This, of course, is inconsistent with capital budgeting and accrual accounting. To this extent both the administrative budget and consolidated cash budget data are inadequate for a set of capital budget accounts. However, since they are the only data available, this particular shortcoming must be overlooked in appraising the capital budget models examined in this study.

The Inclusion of Defense Assets

Certain defense assets are not significantly different from similar nondefense assets. It is not difficult to think of alternative uses for some defense assets in the private sector of the economy or in the nondefense agencies of the government. On the other hand, there are other defense assets for which alternative uses in either the private sector or in nondefense government agencies are limited. Moreover, because these assets are so susceptible to obsolescence or to destruction at any moment of time, it is a formidable challenge to estimate their useful lives with any reasonable degree of certainty.

Since the largest dollar amount of military assets are those which fall into the specialized, destructible category, the most practical alternative is to exclude *all* expenditures for military assets from the capital account. It should be recognized, however, that this policy would exclude a proportionately small amount of expenditures for assets that would be included in the capital account if they had been undertaken by one of the civilian agencies of the government.

Capital Budget Models: Description and Findings

Models I to VII, and the modifications of these models in Appendix F, present a wide range of choices for a capital budget. However, an evaluation of these models, with respect to certain basic issues, leads to the conclusion that only a few of the alternatives represent realistic choices. The other alternatives incorporate one or more features that are unacceptable as the basis for a federal capital budget.

These particular features are also responsible for the widely varying results reflected in Chart I. This chart shows expenditures and receipts for the administrative and consolidated cash budgets and for the current accounts of the seven model capital budgets. It also provides a comparison of budget and current account surpluses and deficits. It illustrates, for example, that in some years deficits in one model examined in this study become surpluses in another model. The cumulative results are even more striking. For instance, had there been a capital budget over the nine-year period covered in this study, a cumulative administrative budget deficit of $31.5 billion would have been converted to a cumulative current account deficit of $12.2 billion (Case II) or to a surplus of between $20.8 billion and $26.4 billion (Case III or Case IV).

Case I

All expenditures for national defense, including those for atomic energy and certain other defense-related activities, are allocated to the current account. Ony federal civil expenditures for real and financial assets owned by the government and certain capital-type receipts (such as loan repayments and proceeds from the sale of government assets) are considered capital items and segregated from the rest of the administrative budget. All government outlays that fall into this classification are included in the capital account regardless of whether they are productive, self-liquidating, nonrecurring, etc. In Case I, no allowance is made for depreciation on new or existing assets nor is any allowance made for losses on loans. Case I, therefore, is a simple descriptive type of capital budget which merely separates (civil) expenditures by duration of benefit. The findings with regard to Case I were:

1. The Case I current account deficits in fiscal years 1955, 1958, 1959, 1961, 1962 and 1963 are significantly below the figures shown in the administrative budget. Similarly, the current account surpluses in fiscal years 1956, 1957 and 1960 are significantly above the figures currently shown in the administrative budget. In no instance, however, does the separation of current from capital receipts and expenditures produce a surplus in the current account for any year that originally had an administrative budget deficit.

2. During the period fiscal years 1955 to 1963, gross civil capital expenditures are not a stable component of adjusted administrative budget expenditures, fluctuating from a high of 15.0 percent in 1955 to a low of 7.5 percent in 1961. In large part, this variation reflects sizable fluctuations of net expenditures for major commodity inventories and loans and financial investments.

3. Since fiscal year 1957, civil investment in social capital and nonfederally-owned assets increases steadily both in absolute amount and as a percent of administrative budget expenditures. Expenditures for civilian research and development account for much of the increase, reflecting the rapid rise of the space program.

Case II

The second model carries capital budgeting beyond the descriptive stage by providing estimated allowances for depreciation on new and previously-acquired assets and for losses incurred on government loans. This model more closely resembles private capital budgeting procedures. As in Case I, the concept of capital includes only those federally-owned items of a civil nature and excludes all national defense expenditures and related receipts. Case II findings were as follows:

1. Adjusting the Case I figures by making an allowance for estimated depreciation and related charges results in higher Case I current account deficits (or lower surpluses) by more than $1 billion in each of the years covered. As in Case I, however, the current account deficits in fiscal years 1955, 1958, 1959, 1961, 1962 and 1963 are significantly below the administrative

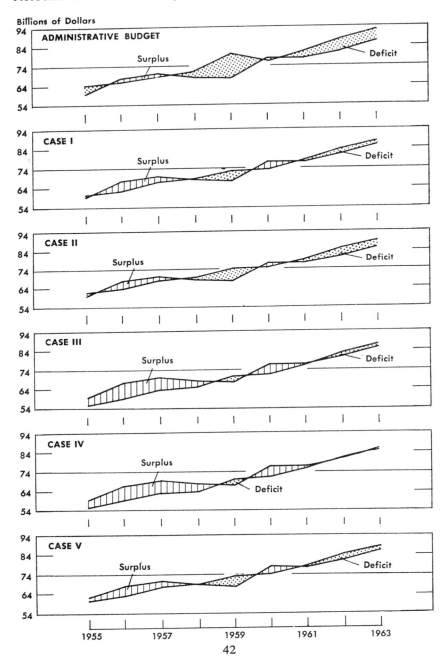

Chart 1, Continued

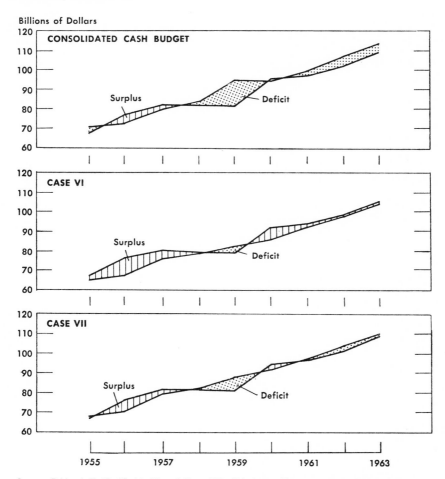

Billions of Dollars

Sources: Tables 6, 7, 11, 15, 16, 19, and 22; and The U.S. Budget (fiscal year 1965), Tables 18 and 19.

budget deficits. The current account surpluses in fiscal years 1956 and 1960 are significantly above the administrative budget surpluses; in fiscal 1957, on the other hand, the current account surplus is slightly less than the administrative budget figure.

2. In no instance does the Case II current account show a surplus for any year that originally had an administrative budget deficit. Even when the current account is adjusted to reflect the

exclusion of federal expenditures for nonfederally-owned assets, there is no year when an administrative budget deficit is changed to a Case II current account surplus.

3. Estimated depreciation allowances and losses on loans have fluctuated during the period under study, reflecting in large part the variability of realized losses on Commodity Credit Corporation inventories. In terms of dollar amounts, losses on major commodity inventories and depreciation on machinery and equipment are the dominant items comprising the depreciation and loss allowance category.

Case III

The third model is similar to Case II except that the definition of capital is expanded to include some national defense receipts and expenditures.[5] Case III findings were:

1. When the current account surpluses or deficits are recalculated with capital outlays defined to include selected national defense items, the administrative budget (and Case II) deficits in fiscal years 1955, 1958 and 1961 become Case III current account surpluses. In 1956, 1957 and 1960 the current account surpluses are considerably larger than the administrative budget surpluses for those years.

2. Similarly, the Case III current account deficits in fiscal years 1959, 1962 and 1963 are considerably smaller than the administrative budget deficits for the same years.

Case IV

A modification of the third model, Case IV, incorporates a broader definition of major military equipment in computing capital expenditures. For Case IV it was found that:

1. When the current account surpluses or deficits are recalculated with capital outlays defined to include a broader list of national defense items, the administrative budget (and Case II)

<hr>

[5] The national defense category used in the present U.S. budget includes the military functions of the Department of Defense, military assistance, the Atomic Energy Commission, and certain other defense-related activities, such as stockpiling of strategic and critical materials.

deficits in fiscal years 1955, 1958, 1961 and 1963 become Case IV current account surpluses.

2. During the period fiscal years 1955 to 1963, with the exception of 1955 and 1956, the current account surpluses under the broader definition of capital military equipment are larger than the comparable figures under Case III assumptions. In two out of three years, that is, 1962 and 1963, the deficits are smaller than had been computed under Case III assumptions; in 1963, a Case III deficit actually becomes a Case IV surplus. In 1959 the Case IV deficit is slightly larger than the Case III deficit.

3. From 1955 to 1960, added depreciation charges and added capital (lower current) expenditures under Case IV assumptions are within $700 million of one another. It is not until fiscal year 1961 that added capital expenditures begin to exceed added depreciation charges by a substantial amount. This seems to indicate that the major increase in defense capital, other than military ships and aircraft, occurred in the 1961-63 period.

Case V

The fifth model resembles Case II except that it provides an estimate of depreciation and related charges only for assets acquired subsequent to fiscal year 1954. In so doing, it assumes that all capital assets acquired prior to fiscal year 1955 were completely written off at the time of acquisition. The findings for Case V were:

1. When the surpluses or deficits are calculated for the current account the current account deficits are significantly below the figures shown in the administrative budget; the current account surpluses are significantly above the figures shown in the administrative budget.

2. In spite of the fact that an allowance for depreciation and related charges is provided only for assets acquired since 1955, in only one year, 1955, does the separation of receipts and expenditures into current and capital accounts produce a surplus in the current account for a year showing an administrative budget deficit.

3. However, when the Case V current account is adjusted to exclude federal expenditures for nonfederally-owned assets, the administrative budget deficits in 1958 and 1961 are also changed

to current account surpluses. In other years, the administrative budget deficits (or surpluses) are considerably lower (higher).

4. Whereas Case II depreciation and related charges increase by about 20 percent over the period 1955 to 1963, they increase by more than 70 percent over the same period under Case V assumptions.

Case VI

The sixth model is based on the consolidated cash budget concept. Thus, it includes the capital transactions of trust funds as well as the general funds of the administrative budget. The scope of the capital account is further broadened to encompass federally-financed assets that are owned by state and local governments and private individuals.[6] As in Case I, no allowance is made for depreciation or related charges. It was found for Case VI that:

1. With only one exception, 1959, the separation of current from capital cash receipts and payments produces a surplus in the current account in every year that originally had a consolidated cash budget deficit.

2. Nondefense cash capital payments average more than 25 percent of total nondefense cash payments over the period 1955 to 1963.

Case VII

Case VII is similar to Case II except that it is based on the consolidated cash budget. In both models only federal civil expenditures are included in the capital account. For Case VII the findings were that:

1. The Case VII current account deficits in fiscal years 1955, 1958, 1959, 1961, 1962 and 1963 are decreased significantly below the figures shown in the consolidated cash budget. Similarly, the current account surpluses in fiscal years 1956 and 1960 are significantly above the figures currently shown in the

---

[6] In Appendix F, several of the other models examined in this study are adjusted to reflect the exclusion from the current account of federal expenditures for nonfederally-owned assets.

consolidated cash budget, and in 1957 the current account surplus is slightly above the cash budget figure. In no instance, however, is there a current account surplus for any year that originally had a cash budget deficit.

2. Adjusting this model for the exclusion of federal expenditures for nonfederally-owned assets changes a cash budget (or an original Case VII current account) deficit to a current account surplus in only one of the years covered, 1955.

3. In each year when there is a consolidated cash deficit, except for 1959 and 1962, the amount of nondefense capital cash expenditures (excluding loan repayments) is considerably more than the amount of the consolidated cash deficit. For the entire period, fiscal years 1955 to 1963, cash expenditures for the acquisition of federally-owned capital and financial assets exceed the cumulative net consolidated cash deficit by nearly $15 billion. As a general conclusion, for the entire nine-year period, federal nondefense cash outlays for capital assets which would either be repaid or yield substantial benefits and services in the future exceed significantly the cumulative consolidated cash deficits incurred. The conclusion is also valid for each of the preceding capital budget models when compared with the administrative budget, and is even more positive for Case III and Case IV where defense as well as nondefense expenditures are included in the capital account.

4. After adjusting cash capital expenditures for such factors as depreciation, obsolescence, repayment of loans, and sales of assets, net nondefense capital outlays during the period 1955 to 1963 are $20.1 billion as compared to a net cash deficit of $22.1 billion, or only $2.0 billion less.

Appraisal of Capital Budget Models

From the description of the capital budget models examined in this study it is understandable why several of them fail to satisfy many of the points discussed above. For example, the Case I model is not a suitable choice because it does not include an allowance for depreciation or related charges. In effect, therefore, it is merely representative of an informational or descriptive type of capital budget which tells us little, if any, more than what is already shown in Special Analysis D[7] of the U.S. budget.

The Case III and Case IV models provide an allowance for depreciation and related charges, but both include some or all military assets in the capital account. These models, therefore, incorporate a broader concept of capital than is desirable for a federal capital budget.

The Case V capital budget model limits its concept of capital to nondefense assets and also provides an allowance for depreciation on these assets. However, the Case V allowances for depreciation and related charges are based only on assets acquired since 1955, the initial year for which data are used in this study. The Case V model does not satisfy the necessary requirements for a budget that would be helpful principally for cost-benefit and cost-trend analysis and for information on net capital formation.

The Case VI model does not provide an allowance for depreciation and related charges; therefore, it too should be eliminated as a desirable form of federal capital budget.

After eliminating several of the models examined in this study, the Case II and Case VII models stand out as the most acceptable and realistic choices for a capital budget statement for the federal government. In each of these models, the capital account includes only nondefense assets that the federal government either owns or in which it has an equity interest or moral responsibility. Each of these models also includes an allowance for depreciation and related charges. Moreover, these allowances reflect the estimated loss or wear and tear and obsolescence on all capital assets including those acquired prior to establishment of the hypothetical capital budget.

Although only Case II and Case VII are realistic models for a federal capital budget, the value of this study would be limited if the estimates for other models were not presented. In part, this study is designed to present material that is useful and relevant to the discussion and evaluation of capital budgeting as a system of accounts for the federal government.

[7] U.S. Bureau of the Budget, Special Analysis D, "Investment, Operating and Other Expenditures," *The Budget of the United States Government* (fiscal years 1957 to 1965).

CHAPTER IV

A Descriptive Capital Budget

THE FIRST MODEL capital budget in the group investigated represents the simplest separation of current and capital accounts. The capital account includes only government-owned nondefense items, and no allowances are made for depreciation or loan losses. It might, therefore, be labelled a descriptive, rather than a functional, capital budget.

Tables 1 to 6 show the results of separating current and capital receipts and expenditures for fiscal years 1955 to 1963. In these tables the intent is to identify and show separately that part of the administrative budget which consists of civil investment in federally-owned assets. They are principally derived from special analyses which have been regularly published in the United States Government Budget.[1]

Capital Expenditures

Tables 1 and 2 are the starting point for all succeeding tables in this study. Table 2 is a summary of the more detailed Table 1.

---

[1] U.S. Bureau of the Budget, Special Analysis D, "Investment, Operating and Other Expenditures," and Special Analysis E, "Federal Credit Programs," *The Budget of the United States Government* (fiscal years 1957 to 1965). Further text references to Special Analysis D and Special Analysis E refer to these documents.

TABLE 1. Federal Administrative Budget Expenditures by Investment Character, Fiscal Years 1955–63[a]

(In millions of dollars)

Expenditure Category	1955	1956	1957	1958	1959	1960	1961	1962	1963
Current operations and expenses	**58,853**	**60,937**	**66,124**	**67,094**	**70,874**	**71,082**	**75,003**	**79,595**	**82,011**
National defense, total	40,695	40,723	43,368	44,234	46,483	45,691	47,494	51,103	52,755
Civil, total	18,158	20,214	22,756	22,860	24,391	25,391	27,509	28,492	29,257
Special aids and services	9,814	11,056	12,917	13,053	14,349	13,625	15,629	16,241	16,109
Agriculture	1,074	1,846	3,564	3,242	3,484	3,458	4,254	5,007	4,675
Veterans	4,375	4,673	4,679	4,898	4,972	4,838	5,017	5,048	5,200
Public assistance grants	1,427	1,455	1,556	1,795	1,966	2,059	2,167	2,432	2,730
International	1,856	1,578	1,646	1,310	1,437	1,323	1,582	1,376	1,126
Post Office	346	462	502	664	736	495	875	722	691
Other	736	1,042	970	1,144	1,754	1,452	1,734	1,656	1,688
Current operating expenses	8,344	9,158	9,839	9,807	10,042	11,766	11,880	12,251	13,147
Interest	6,438	6,846	7,308	7,689	7,671	9,266	9,050	9,198	9,980
Other	1,906	2,312	2,531	2,118	2,371	2,500	2,830	3,053	3,167
Civil investment in social capital and non-federally-owned assets	**1,718**	**1,984**	**1,478**	**1,838**	**2,332**	**3,009**	**3,626**	**4,505**	**6,081**
Research and development	242	305	394	467	669	970	1,409	2,045	3,439
National Aeronautics and Space Administration	43	50	55	72	115	330	646	1,143	2,327
Other	199	255	339	395	554	640	763	902	1,112
Education, training, and health[b]	334	407	483	517	688	837	906	1,049	1,211
Additions to state, local, and private assets	1,098	1,221	543	790	925	1,134	1,247	1,305	1,312
State and local	776	889	149	243	282	298	307	301	376
Private	322	332	394	547	643	836	940	1,004	936

Loans and financial investments[e]........	8,300[d]	6,872[d]	6,071[d]	5,237	8,961[e]	5,423	4,488	6,690	8,054
Public works..........................	1,024	867	1,075	1,252	1,506	1,633	1,874	2,046	2,289
Changes in major commodity inventories...	1,533	1,567	249	515	736	1,023	−390	−1,089	256
Other[f]................................	−234	84	120	123	149	174	363	554	646
Deduct:									
Loan repayments to revolving funds[g].....	6,622[d]	5,771[d]	5,682[d]	4,125	3,859	5,113	2,793	3,884	6,182
Interfund transactions..................	181	315	467	567	355	694	654	633	513
Administrative budget expenditures......	**64,389**	**66,224**	**68,966**	**71,369**	**80,342**	**76,539**	**81,515**	**87,787**	**92,642**

Note: Detail may not add to totals because of rounding.

[a] There are two main sources for the material in this table: Special Analysis D, "Investment, Operating, and Other Expenditures" and Special Analysis E, "Federal Credit Programs," *The Budget of the United States Government.* Figures have been revised to reflect changes in the national defense classification.

[b] Excludes books, records, manuscripts, etc., of the Library of Congress and the Federal Courts (see footnote f).

[c] Loans and investments consist of five major components: (1) major loan programs, (2) minor loan programs, (3) financial investments, (4) net extensions of sales credits and (5) net loan activities in foreign currencies. Data on financial investments are from Special Analysis D. All other data are from Special Analysis E. The major programs, as shown in that analysis, are on a gross basis while the minor programs are included net. Financial investments are also shown net. The adjustment for foreign currencies is the excess of foreign currency loan disbursements over repayments. This adjustment is necessary because foreign currency transactions are not charged to appropriations or funds and are not included in Special Analysis D or the budget totals. An adjustment for net extensions of sales credit is made for the same reason.

[d] Includes $1,920 million of Federal Intermediate Credit Bank loans in 1955; $1,965 million in 1956; and $1,078 million in 1957. In later years (beginning January 1, 1957) the Federal Intermediate Credit Banks became partly privately-owned and their transactions carried as government-sponsored enterprise (trust fund) expenditures. For the same years, loan repayments include $1,857 million, $1,921 million, and $1,229 million respectively for the Federal Intermediate Credit Banks.

[e] Includes nonrecurring subscription of $1,375 million to International Monetary Fund.

[f] Consists of major equipment and other physical assets (including books, records, manuscripts, etc., of the Library of Congress and the Federal Courts). It should be noted that except for fiscal years 1962 and 1963, major equipment does not include automobiles and office equipment. These items are included in the current expenditure category.

[g] This figure represents total repayments into the revolving fund loan programs. It differs from the total repayments figure in Special Analysis E by the amount of collections on nondefense loans which is deposited into the Treasury as "miscellaneous receipts" and is included as administrative budget receipts.

These tables show the distribution of federal administrative budget expenditures classified by their investment character for fiscal years 1955 to 1963. As indicated in Table 1, the term civil "capital," as defined in this study, includes: (1) loans and investments; (2) public works projects; (3) changes in major commodity inventories;[2] and (4) major equipment and other physical assets. Each of these four categories is a separate classification of expenditure in Special Analysis D. This is a gross capital concept and can be interpreted as approximately representing the federal government's gross contribution to capital formation. It is an overstatement of the government's gross (and net) contribution to capital formation to the extent that the data include the acquisition of existing assets, since the purchase of existing assets is a financial investment as contrasted with the acquisition of new assets which is a real investment.

This model does not define capital so as to take account of depreciation allowances or reserves for losses on loans.[3] Therefore, it does not represent net capital formation by the government.

Civil capital investment, as defined in this section of the study, embraces a federally-owned rather than a federally-financed capital concept. Therefore, it does not include federal expenditures, chiefly in the form of grants-in-aid, for additions to state, local and private physical assets, despite the fact that such assets may be, and in many cases are, similar to those purchased directly by the federal government.[4] Clearly, the federal government has a special in-

[2] The commodity inventories held by the Commodity Credit Corporation and other agencies are consumable supplies. However, they are not purchased for current use but are held for a period of years. For this reason they are treated like investments.

[3] In some instances, budget expenditures are reported net of receipts. This is true for all revolving funds. However, the largest component of expenditures in the capital account that is reported on a net basis is loans. The second largest component reported on a net basis is Commodity Credit Corporation expenditures for agricultural inventories. Although gross loan disbursements and repayments data are available from Special Analysis E, the capital account in Case I is slightly understated to the extent that some capital expenditures, other than loans, are reported net of receipts.

[4] In Chapter VIII, where capital expenditures are discussed on the basis of cash payments to the public, federal expenditures for additions to state, local, and private physical assets are included in the capital account. Also, in Appendix F, the Case II, Case V and Case VII results are adjusted to reflect the inclusion of federal expenditures for nonfederally-owned assets in the capital account.

TABLE 2. Summary of Federal Administrative Budget Expenditures by Investment Character, Fiscal Years 1955–63[a]

(In millions of dollars)

Expenditure Category	1955	1956	1957	1958	1959	1960	1961	1962	1963
National defense operations..........	40,695	40,723	43,368	44,234	46,483	45,691	47,494	51,103	52,755
Civil operations and expenses...........	18,158	20,214	22,756	22,860	24,391	25,391	27,509	28,492	29,257
Civil investment in social capital and nonfederally-owned assets	1,718	1,984	1,478	1,838	2,332	3,009	3,626	4,505	6,081
Deduct: interfund transactions..........	181	315	467	567	355	694	654	633	513
Total current expenditures.............	60,390	62,606	67,135	68,365	72,851	73,397	77,975	83,467	87,580
Civil investment in federally-owned assets...........	10,623[b]	9,390[b]	7,515[b]	7,127	11,352	8,253	6,335	8,201	11,245
Deduct: loan repayments to revolving funds[c]............	6,622[b]	5,771[b]	5,682[b]	4,125	3,859	5,113	2,793	3,884	6,182
Administrative budget expenditures............	64,389	66,224	68,966	71,369	80,342	76,539	81,515	87,787	92,642

Note: Detail may not add to totals because of rounding.
[a] Source, Table 1.
[b] See footnote d, Table 1.
[c] See footnote g, Table 1.

53

TABLE 3. Capital Receipts, Fiscal Years 1955–63

(In millions of dollars)

Type of Receipt	1955	1956	1957	1958	1959	1960	1961	1962	1963
Loan repayments[a]	6,894	6,064	5,997	4,442	4,287	5,543	3,235	4,179	6,799
Sale of government property:[b]									
Real property	11	14	16	18	20	20	8	58	135
Scrap, surplus property, etc.	75	153	52	37	44	67	61	28	−61
Sale of vessels[c]	68	85	81	38	38	39	42	27	17
Total capital receipts	7,048	6,316	6,146	4,535	4,389	5,669	3,346	4,292	6,890

[a] These figures are from U.S. Bureau of the Budget, Special Analysis E, "Federal Credit Programs," *The Budget of the U.S. Government*.

[b] Figures on sale of government property are from statements of miscellaneous receipts accompanying the U.S. Budget (fiscal years 1957 through 1965).

[c] For purposes of simplification, these receipts are all considered as coming from civil sources, even though in the years shown a small part of them stem from sale of military assets.

terest in these nonfederally-owned projects. These expenditures, however, are excluded from this statement of a federal capital budget on the grounds that the government does not have complete, and in most cases any, control over the use of these assets during the period in which they will be providing benefits and services. Although these expenditures are not included in the Case I capital account, they are shown as a separate entry in the current account (Table 1) in order to highlight the nature of the assets and to help provide a complete picture of the government's contribution to the nation's gross capital formation.

Also excluded from the definition of capital expenditures but shown as a separate entry in the current account are civil investment expenditures in "social (or human) capital." While not a capital outlay in the general or accounting senses, these expenditures represent a part of the government's contribution to the nation's wealth and productivity. They have the effect of adding to the nation's level of knowledge and skill, and thereby help to increase the capacity to produce a greater national income in future years.

Capital Receipts

As shown in Table 3, capital receipts consist chiefly of loan repayments to revolving funds plus those repayments deposited directly into miscellaneous receipts. These figures are obtained from Special Analysis E. In addition to loan repayments, other capital receipts consist of sales of real and personal property and sales of scrap and salvage materials. Data on these receipts are obtained from annual tables published as supporting material for the miscellaneous receipts table in the U.S. budget document.

Because the published miscellaneous receipts data do not distinguish between sales of products from public lands that were purchased outright and lands that were acquired without payment,[5] or between sales of products that were on the land when acquired and products that were produced later, no distinction between these categories could be made. The capital receipts account is slightly understated to the extent that miscellaneous budget receipts include sales of original timber growth, minerals, and other products from

[5] Perhaps through donation, treaty, conquest, etc.

public lands, since these receipts are not included in the capital account.

Capital receipts are also slightly understated because certain receipts are netted against expenditures in the budget.[6] The major category of capital receipts that is netted against expenditures is gross loan repayments. These can be identified from Special Analysis E, however, so that the extent of understatement is minor.

Finally, capital receipts are understated because a portion of the revenue from income-producing assets (e.g., federal power activities) is not assigned to the capital account. Of course, capital receipts are understated for this reason only when the current account does not include an allowance for depreciation, which is the situation under Case I assumptions. If the current account included an allowance for depreciation (as in Case II, for example), this allowance would already reflect the payments of principal and interest on the previous borrowing for capital items.

Major Findings

The separation of accounts in the Case I model capital budget permits several observations about the character of federal expenditures during the period studied, and the surpluses or deficits that might have occurred in the current account under such a budgetary system.

Stability of Capital Expenditures

Gross civil capital expenditures—the amount of capital expenditures toward which capital receipts could be separately applied—are not a stable component of adjusted[7] federal administrative budget expenditures, in either absolute or relative terms. Table 4 shows that during the 1955 to 1963 period gross civil capital expenditures fluctuated from a high of 15.0 percent in fiscal year 1955 to a low of 7.5 percent of adjusted administrative budget expenditures in 1961. Gross civil capital expenditures by the fed-

---

[6] See footnote 3.

[7] Administrative budget expenditures are presently compiled net of loan repayments. It is necessary, therefore, to increase budget expenditures by the amount of these loan repayments in order to make a meaningful comparison with capital expenditures which are gross of loan repayments. Alternatively, capital expenditures could have been adjusted downward for the loan repayments.

TABLE 4. Gross Civil Capital Expenditures as a Percent of Adjusted Administrative Budget Expenditures and Civil Current Expenditures, Fiscal Years 1955–63[a]

(Dollar amounts in millions)

Fiscal Year	Adjusted Administrative Budget Expenditures[c]	Adjusted Civil Current Expenditures[c]	Gross Civil Capital Expenditures[b]		
			Amount	Percent of Adjusted Administrative Budget Expenditures	Percent of Adjusted Civil Current Expenditures
1955	$71,011	$26,317	$10,623	15.0%	40.4%
1956	71,995	27,654	9,390	13.0	34.0
1957	74,648	29,449	7,515	10.1	25.5
1958	75,494	28,256	7,127	9.4	25.2
1959	84,201	30,227	11,352	13.5	37.6
1960	81,652	32,819	8,253	10.1	25.1
1961	84,308	33,274	6,335	7.5	19.0
1962	91,671	36,248	8,201	8.9	22.6
1963	98,824	41,006	11,245	11.4	27.4

[a] Source, Table 2.

[b] The adjective "gross" has been used to indicate that all loans are included on a gross basis.

[c] Since principal repayments for many loans are deducted in calculating the total of administrative budget expenditures, this total and total civil current expenditures have been adjusted (i.e., increased) by the amount of such loan repayments.

eral government during fiscal year 1963 were about 11.5 percent of adjusted administrative budget expenditures.

Similarly, gross civil capital expenditures are quite unstable as a ratio to adjusted civil current expenditures. During the period 1955 to 1963, gross civil capital expenditures fluctuated from a high of 40.4 percent in 1955 to a low of 19.0 percent of adjusted civil current expenditures in 1961. Gross civil capital expenditures were about 27.5 percent of adjusted civil current expenditures in 1963.

In large part, the wide fluctuation in the amounts of civil capital outlays reflects sizable changes in net budget expenditures for major commodity inventories—mainly farm commodities under the farm price support program. Table 1 shows that these expenditures were about $1.5 billion during fiscal years 1955 and 1956, but dropped sharply to about $250 million during fiscal year 1957 and $515 million in 1958. Net commodity inventory additions then rose to $1 billion in 1960 only to drop $1.4 billion, resulting in net receipts or negative expenditures of $400 million by the end of fiscal year 1961. This category of expenditures continued to fall sharply during 1962, but there was another sharp reversal during fiscal year 1963 and expenditures increased to about $255 million.

Another factor accounting for considerable fluctuation in gross civil investment outlays is the yearly variation of federal expenditures for loans and financial investments. These expenditures, as shown in Table 1, dropped noticeably from 1955 to 1958. They rose sharply from 1958 to 1959, reflecting a nonrecurring subscription in 1959 to the International Monetary Fund, and then dropped sharply again in 1960 and 1961. Expenditures rose significantly again from fiscal year 1961 to 1963 as loans by the Commodity Credit Corporation and the Agency for International Development increased sizably.

In part this reflects a change in the scope of the administrative budget. In fiscal years 1955, 1956 and the first half of 1957, the expenditures of the Federal Intermediate Credit Banks were classified as budget funds; in subsequent years, these expenditures are classified as trust or government-sponsored enterprise funds and are not included in the administrative budget.

Growth in Expenditures for Social Capital and Nonfederal Assets

As shown in Table 5, civil investment in social capital and nonfederally-owned assets has increased steadily since fiscal year 1957 both in absolute amount and in proportion to administrative budget expenditures and current civil expenditures.[8] In fiscal year 1957, such investment amounted to $1.5 billion or 2.1 percent of administrative budget expenditures. In fiscal year 1963, civil investment in social capital and nonfederally-owned assets was $6.1 billion or 6.6 percent of administrative budget expenditures. Similarly, civil investment in social capital and nonfederally-owned assets was 6.2 percent of civil current expenditures in fiscal year 1957 and 17.5 percent in 1963.

All of the components of civil investment in social capital and

[8] For this comparison it is unnecessary to adjust administrative budget expenditures for the amount of loan repayments because gross and net civil investment in social capital and nonfederally-owned assets are the same.

TABLE 5. Civil Investment in Social Capital and Nonfederally-Owned Assets as a Percent of Administrative Budget Expenditures and Civil Current Expenditures, Fiscal Years 1955–63[a]

(Dollar amounts in millions)

Fiscal Year	Administrative Budget Expenditures	Civil Current Expenditures	Civil Investment in Social Capital and Nonfederally-Owned Assets		
			Amount	Percent of Administrative Budget Expenditures	Percent of Civil Current Expenditures
1955	$64,389	$19,695	$1,718	2.7%	8.7%
1956	66,224	21,883	1,984	3.0	9.1
1957	68,966	23,767	1,478	2.1	6.2
1958	71,369	24,131	1,838	2.6	7.6
1959	80,342	26,368	2,332	2.9	8.8
1960	76,539	27,706	3,009	3.9	10.9
1961	81,515	30,481	3,626	4.4	11.9
1962	87,787	32,364	4,505	5.1	13.9
1963	92,642	34,825	6,081	6.6	17.5

[a] Source, Table 2.

nonfederally-owned assets increased over the period 1955 to 1963. However, Table 1 shows that the category accounting for the principal increase is civilian research and development expenditures, and in particular those expenditures of the National Aeronautics and Space Administration. In 1955, civilian research and development expenditures were about $250 million, or roughly 15 percent of total civil investment in social capital and nonfederally-owned assets. By fiscal year 1963 research and development expenditures were about $3.4 billion, or more than 56 percent of total social capital expenditures.

Budget Surpluses and Deficits

Table 6 presents a summary of receipts and expenditures separated by current and capital account. When the surpluses or deficits are recalculated on a current and capital account basis, the current account deficits in fiscal years 1955, 1958, 1959, 1961, 1962 and 1963 are significantly below the figures shown in the

TABLE 6. Summary of Receipts and Expenditures, by Current and Capital Account, Fiscal Years 1955–63[a]

(In millions of dollars)

Budget Category	1955	1956	1957	1958	1959	1960	1961	1962	1963
Current account									
Expenditures	60,390	62,606	67,135	68,365	72,851	73,397	77,975	83,467	87,580
Receipts	59,785	67,306	70,100	68,138	67,387	77,205	77,108	80,998	85,669
Surplus (+) or deficit (−)	**−605**	**4,700**	**2,965**	**−227**	**−5,464**	**3,808**	**−867**	**−2,469**	**−1,911**
Capital account[b]									
Expenditures	10,623	9,390	7,515	7,127	11,352	8,253	6,335	8,201	11,245
Receipts	7,048	6,316	6,146	4,535	4,389	5,669	3,346	4,292	6,890
Surplus (+) or deficit (−)	**−3,575**	**−3,074**	**−1,369**	**−2,592**	**−6,963**	**−2,584**	**−2,989**	**−3,909**	**−4,355**
Administrative budget surplus (+) or deficit (−)	**−4,180**	**1,626**	**1,596**	**−2,819**	**−12,427**	**1,224**	**−3,856**	**−6,378**	**−6,266**

[a] Source, figures are from Tables 2 and 3, and Table 15, *The Budget of the U. S. Government* (1965).
[b] Capital expenditures and receipts are gross by the amount of loan repayments (including those repayments going directly into miscellaneous receipts).

administrative budget. Similarly, the current account surpluses in fiscal years 1956, 1957 and 1960 are significantly above the figures shown in the administrative budget. In no instance, however, does a current account surplus occur in a year in which there was an administrative budget deficit. As expected, there is no capital account surplus in any year since capital receipts fall considerably short of capital expenditures.

These results are of more than just casual statistical interest. The fact that the separation of current from capital receipts and expenditures does not change a deficit to a surplus is some evidence, although admittedly based on a simple accounting model of a capital budget, that capital budgeting will not necessarily hide budget deficits and therefore encourage increased government spending. This possibility has been the basis for some of the opposition to a federal capital budget in spite of the fact that there has been little if any empirical evidence to support such a position.

The Case I model, however, is not representative of the type of capital budget that has been generally proposed for the federal government. A model which more closely resembles the type commonly proposed would include an allowance for depreciation and related charges on capital assets. The Case II capital budget model discussed in the next chapter is of this type.

CHAPTER V

Allowances for Depreciation

CAPITAL BUDGETING, from a technical accounting viewpoint, implies an accounting framework that makes an annual allowance for the depreciation of physical assets and for losses incurred or likely to be incurred on new or outstanding loans—"deterioration of financial assets." The distinguishing feature of this type of accounting, in contrast to the present practice of the federal government (and also in contrast to the descriptive type of capital budget), is that it charges only the estimated current costs of government programs and operations to the current account of the budget. In terms of a conceptual economic framework, the currently-charged expenditure for any capital asset is not the entire amount of the purchase price, but only the amount of the asset that is consumed or the services rendered by the asset during the current accounting period.

Conceptually, this is a valid system of government accounting and of showing the dollar cost of—or services rendered by—various government programs during the current accounting period. This type of procedure is widely used in corporate accounting. However, unlike a private business, the government does not generally attempt to produce goods for profit. By their very nature, most public goods and services are not produced for direct sale to the private sector, nor are the major functions of government executed through a market economy. Consequently, many of the conceptual problems that are inherent even in business accounting are especially difficult to reconcile for the federal government.

Structure of the Capital Account

In the construction of the Case II capital budget statement, the following problems are considered:

1. How do we define and identify the "package" of federal assets that should be included in the capital budget?

2. What is the value of existing assets included in this package of capital assets?

3. What is the value of current additions to those assets?

4. What are the estimated depreciation and loss allowances for assets included in (2) and (3) above?

Definition of Capital Asset

It is necessary to define or set limits on the scope of capital assets and acquisitions to be included in a separate capital account irrespective of the type of capital statement used. The package of capital assets included in the Case II capital account is the same as that included in Case I. These are (a) loans and investments (gross), (b) public works outlays, (c) changes in major commodity inventories, and (d) major equipment and other physical assets. As in Case I, and for the same reasons, the capital account under Case II excludes such items as additions to state, local and private assets, research and development, and education, training and health expenditures.[1] Again, as in Case I, all expenditures for national defense are treated as current outlays.

Value of Existing Capital Assets

Since the usual accounting approach to capital budgeting records depreciation allowances and losses on loans as a current expense and as a capital receipt, it is necessary to determine reasonable values that can be placed on existing capital assets, no matter how defined, as a basis for estimating annual depreciation and related charges. The descriptive type of capital budget, Case I, did not include depreciation allowances so it was not necessary to

[1] In Appendix F, the Case II results are adjusted to reflect the inclusion of federal expenditures for state, local and private assets in the capital account.

provide an estimate of the value of existing capital assets owned by the government.

It is difficult to compile a complete and accurate inventory of existing government assets. Not only are government property records diffused, but in some cases they are incomplete and inaccurate. Moreover, the accounting problem of whether to use original acquisition cost or current replacement cost complicates the task of reporting and measuring the value of existing assets.[2]

Since the fiscal year 1955 the House Committee on Government Operations has published annually a federal property inventory report which presents a compilation of "assigned values of real and personal property owned or controlled by the federal government."[3] The cost figures used in these reports are generally original costs if they are available, or estimates of original costs if they are not. Public domain lands and a small amount of other real property are recorded at estimated present-day values.

The categories of assets reported in the federal inventory reports are broad and in some cases are classified by government organization unit rather than by type of asset. Nevertheless, for the purpose of this study, these categories are adequate, despite the need for some guesswork, for estimating the value of the government's property base for depreciation purposes.

The general classifications that are used in the inventory reports on existing capital assets and their rough equivalent in Special Analysis D,[4] the source for new capital expenditures, are (a) buildings, structures and facilities and (b) machinery and equipment.[5] Changes in major commodity inventories, principally for the Commodity Credit Corporation, are classified as part of the capital

---

[2] For the purpose of its own capital budget, the Swedish government uses replacement cost to determine the value of its capital assets for computing depreciation allowances. It requires all private businesses, however, to use acquisition cost for tax accounting purposes.

[3] *Federal Real and Personal Property Report (Civilian and Military) of the United States Government Covering Its Properties Located in the United States, in the Territories, and Overseas,* House Committee on Government Operations, Committee Print.

[4] U.S. Bureau of the Budget, "Investment, Operating and Other Expenditures." *The Budget of the United States Government,* (fiscal years 1957-65). Further text references to Special Analysis D refer to this document.

[5] Comparable categories in Special Analysis D are (a) public works, and (b) major equipment and other physical assets.

account. Except for a small amount of emergency civil defense supplies, it is not necessary to calculate a loss allowance separately since an allowance for realized losses on farm price support programs is officially estimated each year by the Department of Agriculture. Although the federal inventory reports also contain data on the amount of outstanding loans, anticipated loss allowances on government loans are estimated by a method that does not require the use of such data.

One limitation of the annual inventory reports has been their incomplete coverage of federal real and personal property. This is particularly true of the earlier reports. However, as more and more reports have been compiled through the years, the staff of the Committee on Government Operations, together with department and agency representatives working with the staff, have very closely studied the inventory accounting systems employed by the federal departments and agencies. In doing so, an effort has been made to include assets not previously included in the inventory because of incomplete property records or because inventories were not under accounting control.

Another limitation of the inventory reports is the listing of assets without allowing for depreciation or obsolescence. There are unquestionably many assets reported in the inventory that would or should have been fully depreciated had conventional business accounting practices been in effect.[6] However, since the inventory reports do not indicate the dates of acquisition, it is impracticable to attempt an identification of those assets which technically should be excluded from the property base for depreciation purposes.

Finally, using the inventory reports to construct a base for computing depreciation and related charges does not provide a means for estimating an allowance for the remaining undepreciated value of assets that have been destroyed, sold or given away by the government. In cases of this sort, business accounting procedures normally provide an allowance in the current account to reflect the remaining undepreciated value minus all receipts from sales of such

[6] Although current tax laws permit the use of accelerated depreciation, the conventional principles of business accounting consider depreciation to be a method of spreading the cost of an asset over its useful life. The federal assets reported in the inventory, which should have been fully depreciated would be those assets that outlived their expected life.

assets. Failure to do so understates current account expenditures for the year in which the asset is either destroyed, sold or given away.[7] Thus, on the one hand the inventories in the earlier years are incomplete in coverage, and in all years do not provide a means for estimating the remaining undepreciated value of assets disposed of during the current accounting period. On the other hand they include some assets that should have been fully depreciated before the period under study.

From a strict accounting standpoint, it is not necessary to be concerned with existing assets. Under current government accounting practices, the acquisition cost of all existing assets has, or should have been, fully charged against previous current operating budgets. But economic considerations would require the inclusion of assets in the depreciation base as long as they are still in use. A distorted picture of the current costs of government operations would emerge if depreciation and loss allowances that are, in fact, attributable to current operations are neglected. It should be recognized and admitted, however, that if allowances for depreciation and related charges on existing assets are included in the model, past budgets cannot reflect what might be considered as "true" costs.[8]

For those more concerned with the formal accounting aspects of a capital budget than the economic considerations involved, the Case V (Chapter VII) estimates of depreciation and related charges are confined to only those assets acquired during the period analyzed in this study, fiscal years 1955 to 1963.

Current Additions to Capital Assets

Estimating the value of current additions to the assets included in the capital account principally involves the task of identifying the particular outlays that are to be included during the current accounting period and relating them to the capital stocks in the inventory reports. While these data are available from the accounting records of some departments and agencies, they are not reported by these agencies as part of their regular budget schedules.

[7] This problem is relevant for civil as well as defense assets. It is more relevant for the latter, however. Therefore, to the extent that it contributes to an understatement of depreciation allowances in this study, the Case III and Case IV capital budget models are most affected.

[8] This would also be true for Cases III, IV, V and VII discussed later.

Furthermore, the procedure for obtaining the information for Special Analysis D does not provide the coverage or detail that a full cost accounting system with a balance sheet could provide.[9] For this study, nevertheless, it is necessary to use the broad, general expenditure classifications of Special Analysis D and to attain as much comparability as possible with the federal inventory reports. The two sources of data are generally comparable for the categories concerned. Although some differences do exist, for the most part they are minor and should not distort the major findings of this study.

Estimating Depreciation and Related Charges

Agency budget and accounting records do not usually contain estimates of annual depreciation allowances or probable losses on loans.[10] The problem of estimating both of these items has to be attacked independently. The point of departure for preparing estimates of depreciation and loss allowances on loans for this study is: (a) the property base as compiled from the federal inventory reports, (b) Special Analysis D and Special Analysis E,[11] (c) a study prepared by Robert Hubbell and Wilfred Lewis, Jr.[12] that estimates in detail the depreciation, obsolescence, and losses on federal government assets for fiscal years 1955 and 1956, (d) a study of federal credit programs prepared for the use of the House Subcommittee on Domestic Finance, Committee on Banking and Currency,[13] and

[9] A study which reviewed the basis for classifying budget expenditures, focusing on the impact of government expenditures on the economy and the current capital nature of expenditures, could provide considerable assistance on this problem. See Peter O. Steiner, "The Classification of Budget Data—A Proposal," (staff report for the Bureau of the Budget, Sept. 1, 1962).

[10] The exceptions are data on assets held by the revolving funds and a few selected agencies, notably the Atomic Energy Commission.

[11] U.S. Bureau of the Budget, "Federal Credit Programs," *The Budget of the United States Government* (fiscal years 1957-65). Further text references to Special Analysis E refer to this document.

[12] Robert Hubbell and Wilfred Lewis, Jr., "Estimates of Depreciation, Obsolescence, and Losses on Federal Assets in the Fiscal Years 1955 and 1956," (staff paper prepared for the Bureau of the Budget, July 1957); and a summary of this paper by the same authors, "Capital Consumption by the Federal Government," *National Tax Journal,* Vol. 12 (March 1959), pp. 22-36. Further text references to the Hubbell and Lewis study refer to this paper.

[13] *A Study of Federal Credit Programs,* Committee Print, 88 Cong., 2 sess. (Feb. 1964).

(e) financial statements of the Veterans Administration and the Federal Housing Administration.

The Hubbell and Lewis study is used principally as a source for determining the various rates of depreciation and related charges that can be applied to the figures derived from Special Analysis D and the federal inventory reports on new and existing tangible assets. The authors of that study developed appropriate depreciation rates for various categories of capital which conceptually correspond very closely to the definition of capital used in this study. For all tangible real assets, the depreciation rates are based on the Internal Revenue Service 1942 *Bulletin F* which is used as a guideline for determining useful lives.

The Hubbell and Lewis study developed appropriate rates of depreciation for each category of capital assets, such as buildings, structures, and machinery and equipment. These took into consideration special features of government investments which would have a particular effect on determining a realistic rate of depreciation for government assets. At the same time, Hubbell and Lewis compiled an implied weighted average rate of depreciation based on the detailed items in each asset category. It is these weighted average rates that are used in the present study as a basis for calculating the amount of depreciation on most types of new and existing government assets. For a few assets, such as Maritime and Coast Guard ships, the specific depreciation rates used in the Hubbell and Lewis study are applied in this study.[14]

In this study, as in the Hubbell and Lewis study, the depreciation rates used assume straight line depreciation. Even if the declining balance method or some form of accelerated depreciation were used, however, it is unlikely that the depreciation figures contained in this study would be significantly altered owing to the slow rate of increase in the total (original cost) stock of assets.

---

[14] Although most of the Maritime ships were acquired during World War II, many of these merchant vessels saw relatively little actual service because they were constructed during the later period of the war. Even those ships that saw service, however, were in relatively good condition when the war ended. Thus, by fiscal year 1955 and later, these ships had several more years of useful service left. In spite of obsolescence which would limit their use for competitive commercial shipping purposes, it is assumed that these ships were generally in such good condition that it is reasonable to take a depreciation allowance for them during the period covered in this study.

Figures for loss allowances on commodity inventories reflect primarily realized loss data obtained from accounting records of the Commodity Credit Corporation (CCC). These data represent the amount included in budget expenditures of the CCC as an allowance for net realized losses sustained as a result of inventory revaluation and sales at less than purchase price.

Two separate sources of data are used as the basis for computing loss allowances on government loans and on properties acquired by the housing agencies in default of direct, insured or guaranteed loans. The principal source of data is *A Study of Federal Credit Programs* prepared for the use of the House Subcommittee on Domestic Finance, Committee on Banking and Currency.[15] This is supplemented by financial statements of the Veterans Administration and the Federal Housing Administration.

Three accounting methods can be used to compute loss allowances on loans: (1) actual losses can be reported; (2) a loss rate can be applied to the amount of loans outstanding each year; or (3) a loss rate can be applied to the amount of loan disbursements made each year. Using the first method, losses are written off at the time they are realized. Following the second method, the probable loss allowance is distributed over the entire life of the loan. Using the third method, the entire loss allowance is written off at the time a loan is made. Although a method similar to the second is used in this study to compute and allocate nearly all depreciation allowances on real and personal tangible property, the third method is used for allocating the estimated loss allowances on loans. This departure from earlier methodology is expedient because the available data are more readily adaptable to computing loss ratios based on loan disbursements rather than on the amount of loans outstanding. In spite of the fact that distributing costs over time is the essence of capital budgeting, it is assumed that this departure in methodology does not significantly change the results obtained in this study.

Major Findings

Table 7 summarizes administrative budget receipts and expenditures after they have been separated into current and capital

[15] *Op. cit.*

TABLE 7. Receipts and Expenditures by Current and Capital Account, Allowing for Depreciation and Related Charges, Fiscal Years 1955–63

(In millions of dollars)

Budget Category	1955	1956	1957	1958	1959	1960	1961	1962	1963
Total current account expenditures	61,634	63,897	68,611	69,693	74,079	74,617	79,229	85,100	89,058
Expenditures[a]	60,390	62,606	67,135	68,365	72,851	73,397	77,975	83,467	87,580
Depreciation and related charges[b]	1,244	1,291	1,476	1,328	1,228	1,220	1,254	1,633	1,478
Current receipts[a]	59,785	67,306	70,100	68,138	67,387	77,205	77,108	80,998	85,669
Surplus (+) or deficit (—)	**−1,849**	**3,409**	**1,489**	**−1,555**	**−6,692**	**2,588**	**−2,121**	**−4,102**	**−3,389**
Capital account expenditures[a]	10,623	9,390	7,515	7,127	11,352	8,253	6,335	8,201	11,245
Total capital receipts	8,292	7,607	7,622	5,863	5,617	6,889	4,600	5,925	8,368
Financial receipts[a]	7,048	6,316	6,146	4,535	4,389	5,669	3,346	4,292	6,890
Depreciation and related charges[b]	1,244	1,291	1,476	1,328	1,228	1,220	1,254	1,633	1,478
Surplus (+) or deficit (—)	**−2,331**	**−1,783**	**107**	**−1,264**	**−5,735**	**−1,364**	**−1,735**	**−2,276**	**−2,877**
Administrative budget surplus (+) or deficit (—)	**−4,180**	**1,626**	**1,596**	**−2,819**	**−12,427**	**1,224**	**−3,856**	**−6,378**	**−6,266**

a Source, Table 6.
b Source, Table 8.

accounts and allowances have been made for depreciation and related charges. Current expenditures and capital receipts prior to the addition of depreciation and related charges are the same as those in Table 6, the summary table for the Case I capital budget. Current receipts and capital expenditures are also from the same source. Depreciation and related charges, recorded as an expenditure in the current account and as a receipt in the capital account, are based on Table 8.

Budget Surpluses and Deficits

Table 7 shows the total surplus or deficit on an administrative budget basis and the recalculated surplus or deficit in the current and capital accounts. As in Case I, when the surpluses or deficits are recalculated after separating current from capital items and making an allowance for depreciation and related charges, the current account deficits in fiscal years 1955, 1958, 1959, 1961, 1962 and 1963 were significantly lower than the administrative budget deficits. Similarly, the current account surpluses in fiscal years 1956 and 1960 were significantly above the figures shown in the administrative budget.

Again, as in Case I, in no instance did the separation of receipts and expenditures into current and capital accounts replace an administrative budget deficit with a surplus in the current account. On the contrary, in fiscal year 1957, the Case II current account surplus was actually less than the administrative budget figure—$1,489 million for the current account surplus as compared with $1,596 million for the administrative budget surplus. In the usual case, capital account deficits either offset surpluses, or add to deficits, in the current account so that the total budget surplus is smaller—or the deficit larger—than the current account component. In 1957, however, capital expenditures were relatively small compared to receipts, creating an unusual capital account surplus. This contributed to, rather than subtracted from, the total budget surplus in this year so that the total exceeded the current account surplus by the amount of the capital account surplus.

As to be expected, the general results obtained in Case I and Case II are similar, but the degree to which current account surpluses were larger and deficits were smaller than the administrative budget surpluses or deficits is less pronounced under Case II as-

TABLE 8. Summary of Depreciation and Related Charges, Fiscal Years 1955–63[a]

(In millions of dollars)

Type of Asset or Program	1955	1956	1957	1958	1959	1960	1961	1962	1963
Federal buildings.............................	83	84	82	84	87	92	100	106	112
Other federal structures and facilities...............	141	149	158	165	173	186	198	216	227
Machinery and equipment.......................	372	367	365	371	385	393	419	419	450
Libraries.................................	76	76	76	77	78	78	79	79	79
Loan programs.............................	36	40	37	42	61	57	94	130	172
Loans..................................	30	29	29	35	51	44	62	70	92
Sales of acquired property.....................	6	11	8	7	10	13	32	60	80
Losses on major commodity inventories............	536	575	758	589	444	414	364	683	438
Total.................................	1,244	1,291	1,476	1,328	1,228	1,220	1,254	1,633	1,478

[a] Source, Appendix A Tables A-1 through A-8. All assets and activities classified under the function of national defense are excluded.

sumptions than it is in the Case I model. Obviously, this was because Case II current account expenditures, unlike Case I, include an allowance for depreciation and related charges.

Again, the results obtained from the Case II model offer some evidence that a federal capital budget would not necessarily conceal budget deficits. While the Case II model is a more realistic approach to the type of capital budget that has been most frequently proposed for the federal government, there are many other assumptions that can be made with regard to asset definitions, scope of coverage, rates of depreciation, etc. Applying some of these assumptions produces results that are significantly different in some cases from those obtained under Case I and Case II assumptions.

Growth in Depreciation and Loss Allowances

As indicated in Table 8, estimated depreciation and related charges in 1963 were about 20 percent higher than they were in 1955. This reflects an increase in depreciation or loss allowances for most categories of assets but particularly for loans, buildings and structures, and machinery and equipment. In terms of dollar amounts, losses on major commodity inventories and depreciation on machinery and equipment were the dominant items comprising the depreciation and loss allowance category. As shown in the table, there was a high degree of variability in the annual allowances for realized losses on major commodity inventories. This was particularly true for Commodity Credit Corporation inventories. The variability of these losses, of course, depends more heavily on circumstances in agricultural production and sales than on long-run trends or objectives.

The rate of depreciation or the loss rate on loans for each asset category of Table 8 is assumed to be the same over the entire period of fiscal years 1955 to 1963.[16] The weighted average rate of depreciation is 2.09 percent per year for federal buildings, 1.65 percent for structures and facilities, 5.16 percent for machinery and equipment (except the ships in the Maritime and the Coast

---

[16] The rate of depreciation or percentage loss rate for each category is noted in Appendix A, Tables A-1 through A-8. These tables also show the values for each particular category of assets included in the so-called "package" of capital items.

TABLE 9. Percentage Distribution of Depreciation and Related Charges, Fiscal Years 1955–63[a]

Type of Asset or Program	1955	1956	1957	1958	1959	1960	1961	1962	1963
Federal buildings................	6.7	6.5	5.6	6.3	7.1	7.5	8.0	6.5	7.6
Other federal structures...........	11.3	11.5	10.7	12.4	14.1	15.2	15.8	13.2	15.4
Machinery and equipment..........	29.9	28.4	24.7	27.9	31.4	32.2	33.4	25.7	30.4
Libraries......................	6.1	5.9	5.1	5.8	6.4	6.4	6.3	4.8	5.3
Loan programs..................	2.9	3.1	2.5	3.2	5.0	4.7	7.5	8.0	11.6
Loans......................	2.4	2.2	2.0	2.6	4.2	3.6	4.9	4.3	6.2
Sales of acquired property.......	.5	.9	.5	.5	.8	1.1	2.6	3.7	5.4
Losses on major commodity inventories..	43.1	44.5	51.4	44.4	36.2	33.9	29.0	41.8	29.6
Total.......................	100.0	100.0	100.0	100.0	100.0	100.0	100.0	100.0	100.0

Note: Detail may not add to totals because of rounding.
[a] Source, Table 8.

74

Guard fleet which are depreciated at an annual rate of 5 percent and 4 percent, respectively), and 3.3 percent for library books shelved in the Library of Congress and federal courts. The assumed loss rate on FHA acquired property is 15 percent and the rate on emergency civil defense supplies is 5 percent. The loss rate for loans varies from a low of 0 percent for the 1947-48 loan to the United Kingdom and .01 percent for Rural Electrification Administration loans and Housing and Home Finance Agency urban renewal loans to a high of 2.5 percent for Small Business Administration loans.[17]

Table 9 shows the percentage distribution of estimated depreciation and related charges by type of asset for the fiscal years 1955 to 1963. During this period, losses on major commodity inventories were generally the largest single component of depreciation and related charges, accounting for about 30 to 50 percent of the total. An indication of the high degree of variability of losses on major commodity inventories is given by the fact that in 1961 they accounted for about 30 percent of total depreciation and loss allowances, in 1962 they accounted for almost 42 percent, and in 1963 they were again down to only 30 percent of the total allowances.

Estimated losses on loans quadrupled as a percent of total charges during the period under study, rising from an estimated 2.9 percent in 1955 to 11.6 percent in fiscal year 1963. The percentage share of allowances for depreciation of machinery and equipment was nearly stable, remaining around 30 percent in most years. Estimated depreciation for federal buildings and structures also remained relatively stable as a percent of total allowances. The percentage share of depreciation allowances on libraries and related assets declined over the full nine-year period.

Table 10 shows depreciation and related charges as a percent of net capital expenditures.[18] With the exception of the years 1957 to 1959, this ratio fluctuated within a relatively narrow range centered on about 40 percent. The wide fluctuation in the ratio during the years 1957 to 1959 and the less irregular movements around 40 percent during the remaining years reflect both the uneven

[17] See Appendix A, Table A-5.
[18] Net capital expenditures are gross capital expenditures less loan repayments. Since depreciation and related charges do not include loan repayments, the most meaningful comparison that can be made is with net capital expenditures.

TABLE 10. Depreciation and Related Charges as a Percent of Net Capital Expenditures, Fiscal Years 1955–63[a]

(Dollar amounts in millions)

Fiscal Year	Net Capital Expenditures[b]	Depreciation and Related Charges			
		Depreciation and Losses on Loans	Losses on Major Commodity Inventories	Total	Percent of Net Capital Expenditures
1955	$3,729	$ 708	$536	$1,244	33.4%
1956	3,326	716	575	1,291	38.8
1957	1,518	718	758	1,476	97.2
1958	2,685	739	589	1,328	49.5
1959	7,065	784	444	1,228	17.4
1960	2,710	806	414	1,220	45.0
1961	3,100	890	364	1 254	40.5
1962	4,022	950	683	1,633	40.6
1963	4,446	1,040	438	1,478	33.2

[a] Source, Table 3, Table 6, and Table 8.
[b] Gross capital expenditures minus loan repayments, including repayments going directly into miscellaneous receipts.

pattern of net federal capital expenditures, which appear to exhibit cyclical as well as secular characteristics, as well as the rather erratic movement of losses on commodity inventories.

For most of the period covered in this study, estimated allowances for depreciation and other related charges were only a fraction—about two-fifths—of net capital expenditures. However, if the future rate of capital outlays were to remain constant, after a period of time these allowances would equal new outlays for depreciable assets and the surplus or deficit in the current account would not be affected by the separation of expenditures into current and capital accounts. On the other hand, if the rate of capital outlays were to decline, after a period of time depreciation and related charges would exceed new outlays for depreciable assets and the surplus in the current account would actually decrease (or the deficit increase) as a result of separating current from capital expenditures.[19]

[19] See James A. Maxwell, "The Capital Budget," *Quarterly Journal of Economics*, Vol. 57 (May 1943), where this point is fully discussed.

As indicated by the results in Table 10, it is probably too much to expect that either of the possibilities discussed above could have taken place within the relatively short period of nine years covered in this study. Nor is it very likely that such developments will take place even in the near future since it appears that capital outlays as defined in Case II will continue to be considerably greater than estimated depreciation allowances for many years to come. However, if future budgets should increase the proportion of expenditures in the current account by placing more emphasis on intangible assets—e.g., expenditures for education, training, health, and research and development—it is possible that depreciation allowances could catch up with capital outlays.

CHAPTER VI

Defense Expenditures in the Capital Account

EACH OF THE PROBLEMS and questions raised by the Case II capital budget model becomes more complicated when defense assets are transferred from the current to the capital account. This is largely because of the unique purpose and design of many defense assets. Although some military assets may be substitutes for civilian goods, the majority of them are highly specialized. This raises substantial doubt as to whether such assets should be classified in the capital account at all,[1] and, if so, how they should be depreciated.

Particular hard goods, such as missiles, rockets, tanks, and so forth, may have useful lives of several years or more in the sense that they provide a continuous deterrent force. It would be almost impossible to estimate their useful lives for depreciation purposes, however, because these assets are subject to a rapid and unpredictable rate of technological obsolescence. Further, those assets categorized as weapons may be destroyed—or consumed—at any time if they should be put to actual use. Finally, since there is little

[1] There is some precedent for classifying military assets on a current-capital basis. A distinction between current and capital expenditures was stipulated for the military budgets by the National Security Act Amendment of 1949 (P.L. 216, Sec. 403).

or no demand by the public for this equipment, there is little basis for estimating a liquidation value for it.

Defense assets are not productive in the same sense as capital assets of the private sector of the economy or of the civilian agencies of the federal government. They are more nearly analogous to final goods that are consumed without making any further contribution to production or national income.

Case III: A Narrow Definition of Military Capital

In the Case I and Case II capital budget models, all expenditures for national defense were classified as current expenses, irrespective of the nature of the goods or services purchased. There are certain defense assets, however, that meet generally most of the accounting requirements of capital budgeting. In addition, there also are several other types of assets that are similar enough to nondefense capital assets that their inclusion in a capital account might be reasonably defended. While the selection of only a few types of defense hard goods may seem to be arbitrary, and it probably is, the choice is not too unreasonable.

The Case III capital budget model classifies certain national defense expenditures as capital assets and includes them in the capital account. In addition, certain receipts from the sale or disposition of the strategic and critical materials stockpile and the repayment of defense production loans are included in capital receipts.

Definition of Military Capital Assets

The national defense category is that now used in the U.S. budget. It encompasses the military functions of the Department of Defense, military assistance to other countries, atomic energy, and other activities directly supporting our defense effort.[2]

The package of capital assets included under Case III capital budget assumptions consists of the same categories as in the two previous capital budget models, but expanded to cover the following defense programs:

---

[2] This definition does not differ materially from the major national security concept used in the budget for earlier years and does not affect the capital concept used in this study.

LOANS. National defense loans, for the period under study, were principally for the expansion of defense production. These loans were made to both domestic private and foreign borrowers. In addition, a number of military assistance loans were made to foreign borrowers.

PUBLIC WORKS. Expenditures for military installations and military-related facilities comprise the entire category of military construction. These are classified as national defense expenditures for public works in Special Analysis D.[3]

CHANGES IN MAJOR COMMODITY INVENTORIES. This category of assets includes three types of commodity inventories: One, the expansion of defense production metals and materials; two, stockpiles of strategic and critical materials; and three, emergency civil defense supplies.[4]

MAJOR EQUIPMENT. The definition of major equipment under Case III assumptions is the most difficult—hence the most arbitrary—of any of the four categories of capital assets. In Special Analysis D, expenditures for most identifiable items of major equipment such as ships, aircraft, machine tools, tanks, missiles, etc., are classified and included in the major equipment category.[5] However, because of the unique purpose and function of most military equipment only aircraft and ships are included in the definition of major equipment in Case III.[6] All other major defense items such as missiles, tanks, guns and ammunition are excluded either because there is no market for these assets in the private sector of the economy, hence no (resale) market value, or because it is too conjectural to estimate a useful life for assets that are subject to a rapid rate of obsolescence or possible destruction.

Plant equipment owned by the Department of Defense is also excluded from the capital account, but for technical rather than

[3] U.S. Bureau of the Budget, "Investment, Operating and Other Expenditures," *The Budget of the United States Government* (fiscal years 1957-65). Further references in the text to Special Analysis D refer to this document.

[4] From fiscal year 1955 to fiscal year 1961 civil defense emergency supplies were classified as nondefense expenditures. Since 1961 they have been classified under national defense.

[5] Except for fiscal years 1962 and 1963, automobiles are excluded.

[6] It is interesting to note that in the early capital budgets of the Republic of India the acquisition of naval vessels and of aircraft for defense purposes was also charged to the capital budget.

conceptual reasons. While the stock (inventory) of plant equipment purchased by the Department of Defense is shown in the federal inventory reports, major equipment components are not itemized in Special Analysis D. Hence, comparable current expenditure figures for plant equipment are not available.

Value of Existing Military Capital Assets

The value of most existing military assets is obtained directly from the federal inventory reports.[7] The general classifications used in the inventory reports are (a) buildings, structures, and facilities (considered comparable to public works in Special Analysis D), (b) weapons and other military equipment in use,[8] and (c) materials and supplies (considered comparable to major commodity inventories in Special Analysis D). The source of gross acquisition figures for expansion of defense production metals and materials and the stockpile of strategic and critical materials is the annual budget documents. Finally, the amount of defense production loan disbursements is from Special Analysis E.[9]

Current Additions to Military Capital Assets

Several sources are used to estimate the value of current additions to military capital assets. The value of current expenditures for changes in major commodity inventories and military construction is from Special Analysis D. The value of current expenditures for loans is from Special Analysis E. Estimated current expenditures for military ships are from the Department of Defense.[10] This report shows comparable historical expenditure data for several

[7] *Federal Real and Personal Property Report of the United States Government,* House Committee on Government Operations, Committee Print. Because of the size, the wide dispersal, and the complexity of the Defense Department, the federal inventory report data for that Department may be more defective for the earlier years covered in this study than for the nondefense parts of the government.

[8] This consists principally of military aircraft and various types of naval ships. The inventory figures for military aircraft were adjusted by Defense Department estimates to eliminate the value of missiles included in the aircraft totals.

[9] U.S. Bureau of the Budget, "Federal Credit Programs," *The Budget of the United States Government* (fiscal years 1957-65). Further text references to Special Analysis E refer to this document.

[10] *Order of Magnitude on Comparative Expenditures by Functional Title,* Department of Defense report, FAD-397, Fiscal Year 1965 (Jan. 19, 1964).

appropriation accounts whose funds are spent for such major military items as missiles, aircraft, ships, construction, and so forth. While data by appropriation account include more than just expenditures for the particular asset described in the account title, the amount not directly reflecting the cost of the capital asset is relatively minor. Informal estimates of Defense Department expenditures for aircraft, including aircraft modifications, were made by the Bureau of the Budget and Department of Defense staff members.

Estimating Depreciation and Related Charges on Military Capital Assets

The Hubbell and Lewis[11] study is the principal source of the estimates of depreciation rates for tangible assets and probable loss rates on defense loans. As in Case II, implied weighted average rates of depreciation, based on detailed items for each asset category, are used to compute the estimated depreciation allowances.

The estimated loss allowance on expansion of defense production loans is obtained by applying a 10 percent loss rate, taken from the Hubbell and Lewis study, to gross annual disbursements. The disbursements data are obtained from Special Analysis E.

The estimated loss on the inventory stockpile of strategic and critical materials reflects the actual cost of rotating the inventory. This is based on a rotation procedure used to keep the inventory in usable condition. Since the inventory is not for resale, the cost of rotation approximates the annual cost of the program. The cost figures are obtained directly from annual budget documents.

For the metals and materials stockpile under the Defense Production Act, an 11 percent loss allowance is estimated in the year of acquisition of the stocks. Thus, 11 percent of the value of each year's gross acquisitions is taken as a loss allowance for that year. Since 1955 annual losses on sales have run as high as 25 percent (in 1963) and as low as 2 percent (in 1957), with an (unweighted) average loss per year of 11 percent.

[11] Robert Hubbell and Wilfred Lewis, Jr., "Estimates of Depreciation, Obsolescence, and Losses on Federal Assets in the Fiscal Years 1955 and 1956" (staff paper prepared for the Bureau of the Budget, July 1957). Later references in the text to the Hubbell and Lewis study refer to this paper.

Estimates For the Atomic Energy Commission

The procedure for estimating annual capital expenditures, depreciation and related charges for the atomic energy program is greatly simplified by the proficient accounting records and practices of the AEC. As part of its regular accounting records, the AEC shows costs incurred annually for plant and equipment and annual depreciation charges. The depreciation charges reflect the "net total of periodic credits for the amortization of the cost of completed plant and equipment. . . . [It] represent[s] the allocation to each period of the costs of units or groups of units of depreciable plant and equipment plus estimated costs and less estimated salvage credits, if any."[12] The costs incurred for plant and equipment include the costs of design, construction or other acquisitions of land, property rights, roads, buildings, other structures, utility lines, and equipment that are expected to have a useful service life longer than one year. The AEC provided a historical series for both annual capital expenditures and estimated depreciation charges for the fiscal years 1955 through 1963. The data used in the present study are based on these estimates.

Budget Surpluses and Deficits

Table 11 summarizes administrative budget receipts and expenditures after separating them into current and capital accounts and after adjusting them for national defense expenditures of a capital nature and the applicable depreciation and related charges. The table also shows the administrative budget surplus or deficit recalculated into the surplus or deficit in both the current and capital accounts as defined for this case. Two interesting observations can be made from this table. The first is that when the surpluses or deficits are recalculated for the current account the administrative budget (and Case II current account) deficits in fiscal years 1955, 1958 and 1961 became current account surpluses. This finding differs notably from the results obtained under Case I and Case II assumptions where all national defense expenditures are classified as current outlays. In these models, in years showing

[12] U.S. Atomic Energy Commission, *Accounting Handbook,* Part I, Appendix 1101, Section B, Account No. 2200 (1962), p. 14.

TABLE 11. Receipts and Expenditures by Current and Capital Account, Including National Defense Expenditures, Fiscal Years 1955–63

(In millions of dollars)

Budget Category	1955	1956	1957	1958	1959	1960	1961	1962	1963
Total current account expenditures	55,761	59,339	63,950	64,572	70,359	71,686	76,810	82,881	86,754
Expenditures[a]	50,688	53,628	57,780	58,102	63,828	64,906	69,935	75,260	79,045
Depreciation and related charges	5,073	5,711	6,170	6,470	6,531	6,780	6,875	7,621	7,709
Nondefense capital assets[b]	1,244	1,291	1,476	1,328	1,228	1,220	1,254	1,633	1,478
Defense capital assets[c]	3,829	4,420	4,694	5,142	5,303	5,560	5,621	5,988	6,231
Current Receipts[a]	59,741	67,257	70,050	68,090	67,320	77,099	76,956	80,906	85,464
Surplus (+) or deficit (−)	**3,980**	**7,918**	**6,100**	**3,518**	**−3,039**	**5,413**	**146**	**−1,975**	**−1,290**
Total capital account expenditures	20,325	18,368	16,870	17,390	20,375	16,744	14,375	16,408	19,780
Nondefense[a]	10,623	9,390	7,515	7,127	11,352	8,253	6,335	8,201	11,245
Defense[d]	9,702	8,978	9,355	10,263	9,023	8,491	8,040	8,207	8,535
Total capital receipts	12,165	12,076	12,366	11,053	10,987	12,555	10,373	12,005	14,804
Financial receipts	7,092	6,365	6,196	4,583	4,456	5,775	3,498	4,384	7,095
Nondefense[a]	7,048	6,316	6,146	4,535	4,389	5,669	3,346	4,292	6,890
Defense[e]	44	49	50	48	67	106	152	92	205
Depreciation and related charges	5,073	5,711	6,170	6,470	6,531	6,780	6,875	7,621	7,709
Nondefense capital assets[b]	1,244	1,291	1,476	1,328	1,228	1,220	1,254	1,633	1,478
Defense capital assets[c]	3,829	4,420	4,694	5,142	5,303	5,560	5,621	5,988	6,231
Surplus (+) or deficit (−)	**−8,160**	**−6,292**	**−4,504**	**−6,337**	**−9,388**	**−4,189**	**−4,002**	**−4,403**	**−4,976**
Administrative budget surplus (+) or deficit (−)	**−4,180**	**1,626**	**1,596**	**−2,819**	**−12,427**	**1,224**	**−3,856**	**−6,378**	**−6,266**

[a] Source, Table 6. [b] Source, Table 8. [c] Source, Table 12. [d] Source, Table 13. [e] Source, Table 14.

84

an administrative budget deficit, there is a significantly smaller current account deficit, but not a current account surplus.

The second point of note relates to the recalculated surpluses and deficits for fiscal years 1956, 1957, 1959, 1960, 1962 and 1963. In these years, the deficits, when recalculated for the current account, were smaller and the surpluses were larger compared to the figures for the administrative budget, as they were in Cases I and II. However, under Case III assumptions, the reduction of the adjusted current account deficits in fiscal years 1959, 1962 and 1963 was greater than under Case I and Case II assumptions. Similarly, under Case III assumptions, the increase in the adjusted current account surpluses in 1956, 1957 and 1960 was greater than under Case I and Case II assumptions. The relative comparison between the Case III and the Case II current account surpluses in 1957 is even more dramatic because the Case II surplus was found to be less than the administrative budget surplus.

Several factors contribute to these statistical findings. For example, in each of the years in which administrative budget deficits became current account surpluses, that is, fiscal years 1955, 1958 and 1961, the budget deficits were the lowest recorded during the period studied. Thus it is easier for the recalculation of the current account to result in a surplus for any one of these years than it would be for a year such as 1959 when the administrative budget deficit was $12.4 billion.

These statistical findings also largely reflect the direct relationship between changes in the rate of federal capital investment and the current level of depreciation allowances and related charges. Depreciation allowances and related charges under Case III assumptions are greater than for Case II. Although this has the effect of contributing to larger current account deficits, capital outlays during the years noted increased, producing an even larger capital account deficit. Therefore, in all the years covered in this study, the current account results under the Case III assumptions are an "improvement" over the administrative budget surplus or deficit position of the government to a greater extent than under either Case I or Case II assumptions.

In part, increasing costs of military assets during the period studied account for the larger capital outlays. To a greater extent, however, the increase in capital outlays reflects a real net acquisi-

TABLE 12. Summary of Depreciation and Related Charges, National Defense, Fiscal Years 1955–63 [a]

(In millions of dollars)

Type of Asset	1955	1956	1957	1958	1959	1960	1961	1962	1963
Federal buildings and structures........	584	628	687	746	826	890	949	984	1,015
Major military equipment................	2,938	3,490	3,708	4,058	4,152	4,365	4,374	4,694	4,919
Other[b]................................	307	302	299	338	325	305	298	310	297
Total depreciation and related charges	3,829	4,420	4,694	5,142	5,303	5,560	5,621	5,988	6,231

[a] Source, See Appendix B, Tables B-1 through B-6. [b] Consists of changes in major commodity inventories, loan programs, and the Atomic Energy Commission.

TABLE 13. Summary of National Defense Capital Expenditures by Type, Fiscal Years 1955–63 [a]

(In millions of dollars)

Expenditure	1955	1956	1957	1958	1959	1960	1961	1962	1963
Public works[b]........................	1,620	2,076	1,986	1,755	1,943	1,617	1,603	1,319	1,134
Major military equipment..............	6,318	6,088	6,584	7,601	6,506	6,429	5,938	6,386	6,938
Aircraft..............................	5,374	5,230	5,742	6,495	5,015	4,685	4,137	4,480	4,416
Ships................................	944	858	842	1,105	1,491	1,744	1,801	1,906	2,522
Other[c]..............................	1,764	814	785	907	574	445	499	502	463
Total national defense capital expenditures..............................	9,702	8,978	9,355	10,263	9,023	8,491	8,040	8,207	8,535

[a] Data on public works and changes in major commodity inventories are obtained from Special Analysis D (fiscal years 1957–65); data on expansion of defense production loans are obtained from Special Analysis E (fiscal years 1957–65); data on military ships are obtained from Department of Defense report, FAD-397, fiscal year 1965 (19 January 1964); data on military aircraft are estimates made by Bureau of the Budget and Department of Defense staff members; and data for the AEC are obtained directly from the Atomic Energy Commission.
[b] Mainly military construction.
[c] Consists of major commodity inventories, expansion of defense production loans (gross) and capital expenditures of the Atomic Energy Commission.

tion of defense capital assets. It must be remembered, however, that the Case III definition of defense assets is quite restricted since it includes only aircraft and ships in the major equipment category. Thus, any conclusions about the relative status of our defense capital over time must be tempered by this definition.

Depreciation and Loss Allowances

Table 12 summarizes estimated depreciation and loss allowances for national defense capital items.[13] The weighted average rate of depreciation used is 2.85 percent per year for military buildings, structures and facilities, 9.09 percent for military aircraft, 6.67 percent for naval ships and 10 percent for naval craft. The loss rate for expansion of defense production metals and materials inventories is 11 percent while an annual rate of 5 percent is used for inventories of emergency supplies. For expansion of defense production loans, the loss rate used is 10 percent and is applied to annual gross loan disbursements.

As shown in Table 12, the major share of depreciation and related charges was the allowance for wear and tear of military aircraft and ships—major military equipment. This principally reflected the large inventory of existing aircraft and naval ships coupled with the fact that the assumed rate of depreciation for aircraft and ships is relatively high, 9.09 percent and 6.67 percent per year, respectively. The relative proportion that each category of capital assets was of total depreciation charges changed very little over the nine-year period. The greatest change was for the atomic energy program and other defense-related activities which declined from 8.0 percent of total depreciation charges in 1955 to 4.8 percent in 1963.

Case IV: A Broader Definition of Military Capital

In Case III, the definition of defense capital expenditures, and in particular military equipment, was limited to a narrow range of items. Out of all military weapons, only aircraft and ships were included in this definition. This choice of a narrow definition of

---

[13] The rates of depreciation and losses on loans are noted in the footnotes to Appendix B, Tables B-1 through B-7. These tables also show the values for each particular category of capital asset.

TABLE 14. Capital Receipts Other Than Depreciation and Related Charges, National Defense, Fiscal Years 1955–63[a]

(In millions of dollars)

Type of Receipt	1955	1956	1957	1958	1959	1960	1961	1962	1963
Repayment of loans.........	44	45	42	43	62	37	72	39	131
Sale or dispositions from strategic and critical materials stockpile	—	4	8	5	5	69	80	53	74
Total....................	44	49	50	48	67	106	152	92	205

[a] Source, *The Budget of the United States Government* (fiscal years 1957–65), and U. S. Bureau of the Budget, "Statement of Miscellaneous Receipts" (fiscal years 1957–65).

defense capital assets was a compromise solution to the conflict over the conceptual issue of whether any military outlays should be classified as capital assets. This solution was also partly dictated by a lack of basic data.

There is some justification for classifying more military equipment, other than military aircraft and ships, as capital assets even if in doing so a more elementary method must be used to estimate depreciation allowances and current additions to defense capital outlays. The Case IV model was designed as a defensible alternative to the limited range of the Case III model. The basic difference between the two models is the broader definition of the major equipment category of defense capital assumed in Case IV. In addition, however, Case IV capital receipts include the proceeds from the sale of certain defense assets that were not defined as capital or included in Case III receipts.

Definition of Capital

In the Case IV model, military capital is broadened to include all major equipment: equipment issued for use including missiles,[14] all of the production equipment inventory, and major depreciable heavy goods available in the Defense Department supply system inventories including the stock funds.

Data on this equipment are from the federal inventory reports

[14] Even under a broad concept of defense capital it is questionable whether a missile should be counted as a capital asset since it can only be "used" once. However, the available data do not readily permit an identification of the stock of these weapons and, therefore, they are included in this broader concept.

on real and personal property and are used to approximate the depreciation base for the newly-defined category of major equipment. Depreciation allowances are computed for these asset categories using depreciation rates obtained primarily from the Hubbell and Lewis study.[15] The estimate of current capital expenditures is the entire amount of Defense Department expenditures for major equipment as reported in Special Analysis D.[16]

Comparison with Case III Results

Table 15 is designed as a source of modifications to the various Case III tables. It shows (1) added capital (lower current) expenditures, (2) added depreciation allowances, (3) added capital (lower current) receipts, (4) change in the current account surplus or deficit, (5) the original Case III current account surplus or deficit, and (6) the new current account surplus or deficit.

The general results shown in Table 15 closely follow those found in the Case III summary table even though the Case IV concept of defense capital has been broadened. Thus, in fiscal years 1955, 1958 and 1961 when there was an administrative budget deficit, separating current from capital items and making an allowance for depreciation produced a Case IV current account surplus. This was also true in Case III. In addition, however, there was also a change for fiscal 1963 from a deficit under Case III assumptions to a surplus in the Case IV current account.

A comparison of the first two columns of Table 15 reveals an interesting relationship between the added depreciation charges and added capital (lower current) expenditures under Case IV assumptions. From 1955 to 1960, the figures for each of these categories were very close to one another (within $0.7 billion). It is not until fiscal year 1961 that added capital expenditures began to exceed added depreciation charges by a substantial amount, indicating that the major increase in defense capital stock items other

---

[15] See Appendix C, Table C-1.

[16] The "major equipment category" in Special Analysis D (primarily the military procurement account) includes some military expenditures for goods which are for early consumption and are not depreciable. On the other hand, the Special Analysis D category "current expenses for repairs and maintenance" (primarily the military operations and maintenance account) includes some amounts of defense investments for future use. It was assumed that the inclusion of the one group of expenditures in national defense major equipment and the exclusion of the other approximately offset one another.

TABLE 15. Change in Current Account Surplus or Deficit Using a Broader Definition of Major Military Equipment, Fiscal Years 1955–63[a]

(In millions of dollars)

| Fiscal Year | Change in Current Expenditures | | Change in Current Receipts | Net Change in Current Account | Current Account Surplus (+) or Deficit (−) | |
	Added Capital (Lower Current) Expenditures (1)	Added Depreciation Charges (2)	Added Capital (Lower Current) Receipts (3)	(4)=(1)− [(2)+(3)]	Case III (5)	Case IV (6)= (4)+(5)
1955	6,676	6,544	217	−85	3,980	3,895
1956	6,110	6,219	236	−345	7,918	7,573
1957	7,053	6 471	239	+343	6,100	6,443
1958	6,968	6,263	252	+453	3,518	3,971
1959	6,052	6,003	216	−167	−3,039	−3,206
1960	6,312	5,939	197	+176	5,413	5,589
1961	7,062	5,753	152	+1,121	146	1,267
1962	7,919	6,006	97	+1,816	−1,975	−159
1963	8,209	5,828	100	+2,281	−1,290	991

[a] Source, Tables 11, 12 and C-1.

than military ships and aircraft occurred in the 1961-63 period.

There is one other Case IV result that warrants a few words of comment, particularly since it suggests a difference from Case III. As shown in Table 15, in all but three years, 1955, 1956, and 1959, during the period 1955 to 1963, Case IV current account surpluses were larger and the deficits were smaller than the corresponding figures for Case III. In 1963, of course, the more than $1 billion Case III deficit becomes a $1 billion surplus. This seems to indicate that in general, even though in both models there appeared to be an increase in the government's capital stock during the period studied, there was a larger net increase in the nation's defense capital under the broader definition of Case IV than there was under the more restricted Case III assumptions. This indicates that additional capital expenditures under the adjusted concept of depreciable equipment of Case IV are greater than the sum of the additional capital receipts (from the sale, salvage, or scrapping of capital assets) and the additional depreciation allowances.

CHAPTER VII

Depreciation of Assets Acquired Since 1955

IN EACH OF THE PRECEDING models where an allowance is made for depreciation and losses on loans, it was assumed that depreciation was based on all capital assets including those acquired prior to 1955, the year in which the capital budget is established. It may be argued, however, that such assets and a related amount of depreciation and other charges on such assets should not be included in a capital budget model for the federal government because they were written off in the administrative budget accounts at the time they were aquired.

The Case V model is set up in order to see what the results would be if depreciation allowances on federal assets acquired prior to fiscal 1955 were excluded. This model is identical to the Case II model in all other respects. There is no difference between the Case V definition of a capital asset and the Case I or Case II definition. In each case, the definition includes all nondefense additions to federal assets, both real and financial.

Estimating Depreciation and Loss Allowances

The depreciation base, under Case V assumptions, is estimated by cumulating annual budget expenditures as reported in Special Analysis D[1] for each of the following categories: (1) public works, (2) major equipment, and (3) other real assets. Then, for each of these three categories, an appropriate depreciation rate[2] is applied to each year's cumulated total, starting with the fiscal year 1955. Since the study covers only a 9-year period, in no instance is an asset that was acquired in an early year fully depreciated by the end of the ninth year.

It should be noted that this method of determining the depreciation base results in a slightly overstated figure. This is unavoidable because the expenditure figures in Special Analysis D include outlays for work-in-process for which normally no depreciation allowance would be made. Moreover, using this method to approximate the depreciation base does not eliminate the value of assets that were later sold, destroyed or given away and therefore would no longer be included in the government's property inventory.[3]

The estimated loss allowances on major commodity inventories—primarily Commodity Credit Corporation inventories—are computed on the basis of information reported in the annual budget documents. In the case of CCC inventories, the ratio of

[1] U.S. Bureau of the Budget, "Investment, Operating and Other Expenditures," *The Budget of the United States Government* (fiscal years 1957-65). Further references in the text to Special Analysis D refer to this document.

[2] It is assumed that the public works category is comparable to the buildings and structures group in Case II. Thus, for this category, a weighted average annual depreciation rate of 1.8 percent is used. The equipment category consists mainly of Maritime ships plus some Post Office, Treasury (Coast Guard), National Aeronautics and Space Administration and Federal Aviation Agency equipment. A depreciation rate of 5 percent is used for Maritime ships and 5.16 percent for all other equipment (expenditures for Coast Guard ships could not be separately identified). The "other assets" category consists primarily of Department of Agriculture (reclamation, watershed projects, and so on) and Interior projects. For these assets a 2.0 percent depreciation rate is used. These rates are based on Hubbell and Lewis, "Estimates of Depreciation, Obsolescence, and Losses on Federal Assets in the Fiscal Years 1955 and 1956" (staff paper prepared for the Bureau of the Budget, July 1957). The depreciation base and estimated depreciation allowances for these three categories of assets are shown in Appendix D, Tables D-1 through D-4.

[3] This is the other side of the program noted in Chapter V, p. 66.

annual budget loss allowances on inventories to gross inventories on hand at the start of the fiscal year is computed. This ratio is applied to annual gross acquisitions of inventories in order to estimate the loss on current commodity acquisitions. The loss allowance for commodity inventories of emergency civil defense supplies is computed by applying an assumed loss rate of 5 percent, obtained from the Hubbell and Lewis study, to gross annual disbursements.[4]

For the Case V model, probable loss allowances for loans and properties acquired in default of loans are the same as those used in the Case II model. This is consistent with Case V assumptions since these particular losses for Case II were computed on the basis of annual disbursements, and the allowance was taken in the year in which disbursements were made.

Although it is not necessary to recalculate probable losses on loans for the Case V model, it is necessary to adjust loan repayments allocated to the capital receipts account.[5] In order to maintain consistency, if the current account does not include a loss allowance on loans made prior to fiscal year 1955, logically the capital account should not include the repayment of loans made prior to 1955.

For most lending agencies the method for estimating Case V loan repayments is relatively simple. In some cases, the loan program was started after 1954. In these cases, all repayments are allocated to the capital account. This is true for Federal National Mortgage Association (FNMA) special assistance functions, student loans, and area redevelopment loans. In other cases, it is assumed that all repayments over and above an amount equal to the value of loans outstanding at the end of fiscal year 1954 reflect the repayment of loans made since 1955.[6] This seems to be a reasonable assumption since many of the loans made by the government have short average maturities with a frequent turnover.

[4] See footnote 4, Chapter VI, page 80. The estimated loss allowances for major commodity inventories are shown in Appendix D, Tables D-5 and D-6.

[5] Loan repayments, by type of loan or program, for Case V are shown in Appendix D, Table D-7.

[6] The amount of loans outstanding at the end of fiscal year 1954 and annual loan repayments for 1955 to 1963 are obtained from Special Analysis E, U.S. Bureau of the Budget, "Federal Credit Programs," *The Budget of the United States Government,* (fiscal years 1957-65).

The above procedure cannot be used to estimate the probable loss allowances for loan programs that have long-term maturity schedules. This would include the lending programs of the Federal Housing Administration, the Veterans Administration, the management and liquidating functions of the FNMA, the Rural Electrification Administration, the Export-Import Bank, and all of the foreign aid lending agencies. A repayment schedule is estimated for these programs in the following manner. A loan repayment is computed based on an assumed average loan maturity. For example, assuming that Export-Import Bank loans have an average maturity of 15 years, the loan repayment rate is 6.66 percent per year. In the case of Federal Housing Administration, Veterans Administration and FNMA (management and liquidating functions) loans, a 30-year amortization schedule is used to determine the annual repayment rate. The estimated repayment rate is applied to the annual cumulative total of loan disbursements made since fiscal year 1955.[7] This provides an estimate of the annual loan repayments for each particular program, based on the amount of annual gross loan disbursements made since 1955.

One final adjustment is made to the series of loan repayments so derived. When the cumulated estimated repayments equal the amount of loans outstanding at the end of fiscal year 1954, all repayments thereafter are assumed to reflect loans made since 1955.

Major Findings

Case V is intended to show the changes in administrative budget receipts and expenditures after they have been separated into current and capital accounts and allowances have been made for depreciation and related charges only on assets acquired since 1955.

Budget Surpluses and Deficits

Table 16 shows the total surplus or deficit on an administrative budget basis compared with the recalculated surplus or deficit in the current and capital accounts. As in Case I and Case II, when the surpluses or deficits are recalculated for the current account

---

[7] Annual loan disbursements were obtained from Special Analysis E.

TABLE 16. Receipts and Expenditures by Current and Capital Account, Including Depreciation and Related Charges on Assets Acquired Since 1955, Fiscal Years 1955–63.[a]

(In millions of dollars)

Budget Category	1955	1956	1957	1958	1959	1960	1961	1962	1963
Total current account expenditures......	60,811	63,042	67,749	69,139	73,431	74,048	78,492	84,158	88,299
Expenditures[b]......	60,390	62,606	67,135	68,365	72,851	73,397	77,975	83,467	87,580
Depreciation and related charges[c].	421	436	614	774	580	651	517	691	719
Current receipts......	62,277	68,372	70,897	68,940	68,020	78,479	77,768	81,820	86,554
Surplus (+) or deficit (—)......	1,466	5,330	3,148	—199	—5,411	4,431	—724	—2,338	—1,745
Capital account expenditures[b]......	10,623	9,390	7,515	7,127	11,352	8,253	6,335	8,201	11,245
Total capital receipts......	4,977	5,686	5,963	4,507	4,336	5,046	3,203	4,161	6,724
Financial receipts[d]......	4,556	5,250	5,349	3,733	3,756	4,395	2,686	3,470	6,005
Depreciation and related charges[c].	421	436	614	774	580	651	517	691	719
Surplus (+) or deficit (—)......	—5,646	—3,704	—1,552	—2,620	—7,016	—3,207	—3,132	—4,040	—4,521
Administrative budget surplus (+) or deficit (—)......	—4,180	1,626	1,596	—2,819	—12,427	1,224	—3,856	—6,378	—6,266

[a] Total financial receipts and total expenditures are overstated by the amount of (Case I) loan repayments (excluding those repayments going directly to miscellaneous receipts).
[b] Source, Table 6.
[c] Source, Table 17.
[d] Source, Appendix D, Table D-7. It is assumed that all receipts from the sale of assets reflect the disposition of assets acquired before 1955. Therefore they are classified as current receipts.

TABLE 17. Summary of Depreciation and Related Charges for Civil Assets Acquired Since Fiscal Year 1955, Fiscal Years 1955–63

(In millions of dollars)

Type of Asset	1955	1956	1957	1958	1959	1960	1961	1962	1963
Public works[a]	18	34	53	76	103	132	166	203	244
Machinery and equipment[b]	2	4	5	7	10	15	17	23	29
Loan programs[c]	36	40	37	42	61	57	94	130	172
Loans	30	29	29	35	51	44	62	70	92
Sales of acquired property	6	11	8	7	10	13	32	60	80
Losses on major commodity inventories[d]	365	357	518	647	404	444	235	329	267
Other assets[e]	*	1	1	2	2	3	5	6	7
Total	421	436	614	774	580	651	517	691	719

* Less than $500 thousand.
[a] Source, Appendix D, Table D-1.
[b] Consists mainly of assets held by the Maritime Administration, Treasury Department (Coast Guard), Post Office, National Aeronautics and Space Administration, Federal Aviation Agency and Library of Congress. Source, Appendix D, Tables D-2 and D-3.
[c] Source, Appendix A, Tables A-5 and A-6.
[d] Source, Appendix D, Tables D-5 and D-6.
[e] Consists primarily of assets held by the Department of Agriculture and the Department of the Interior. Source, Appendix D, Table D-4.

under the Case V assumptions, the current account deficits were significantly smaller and the current account surpluses were significantly larger than the figures shown in the administrative budget. In spite of the fact that depreciation and related charges are computed only on assets acquired since 1955, in only one instance when there was an administrative budget deficit, fiscal year 1955, did the separation of receipts and expenditures into current and capital accounts produce a surplus in the current account. This occurred because of a combination of large current account receipts and small current account expenditures.

Because of the manner in which they are derived, Case V financial capital receipts (loan repayments) in 1955 were quite small relative to Case I or Case II receipts. Thus, Case V current account receipts—which are derived as a residual—were greater than Case I or Case II current receipts for the same year. Similarly, Case V current account expenditures in 1955 were relatively small because capital outlays in the same year were large.

Growth in Depreciation and Loss Allowances

Table 17 presents a summary of depreciation and related charges for the Case V model. As in the Case II model, losses on major commodity inventories were the dominant component of depreciation and related charges during the period of fiscal years 1955 to 1963. Similarly, they also exhibited the greatest amount of year-to-year fluctuation.

As a percent of total depreciation charges, estimated depreciation on public works projects rose from 4.3 percent in 1955 to 33.9 percent in 1963. As noted earlier, this figure is probably overstated because some assets may have been sold, destroyed or given away and because it includes work-in-process. Nevertheless, it appears that over an extended period of years the depreciation allowances for federal public works would probably dominate total allowances for depreciation and related charges. This assumes, of course, that the definition of a capital asset is not broadened to include, for example, federal investment in "social (or human) capital."

Table 18 indicates the pace at which depreciation and related charges can grow over a short period of time. In this table, depreci-

TABLE 18. Ratio of Case V Depreciation Allowances to Case II Depreciation Allowances, Fiscal Years 1955–63.[a]

(Dollar amounts in millions)

Fiscal Year	Estimated Depreciation and Related Charges		Percent of Case II Charges
	Case II	Case V	
1955	$1,244	$421	34%
1956	1,291	436	34
1957	1,476	614	42
1958	1,328	774	58
1959	1,228	580	47
1960	1,220	651	53
1961	1,254	517	41
1962	1,633	691	42
1963	1,478	719	49

[a] Source, Table 8 and Table 17.

ation and related charges on assets acquired since 1955—the Case V assumption—are compared with similar figures that also include previously acquired assets—the Case II assumption—in the federal property inventory during the period 1955 to 1963. Whereas these charges under Case II assumptions increased by about 20 percent over the period covered in this study, they increased by more than 70 percent over the same period under Case V assumptions. They were still relatively small compared to the depreciation allowances of Case II, however.

In 1955, Case V depreciation allowances were only 34 percent of Case II allowances, and, although there is considerable annual fluctuation, in 1963, the ratio was still only 49 percent. During the entire period studied, the highest ratio was 58 percent (1958).

Consolidated Cash Capital Budgets

THE CAPITAL BUDGET MODELS examined thus far in this paper are based on the administrative budget and define only federally-owned assets as capital. Therefore, they do not reflect as capital investment several significantly large programs outside of the administrative budget. For example, the highway trust fund since 1959 has been adding to the nation's stock of capital assets at an average rate of about $2.9 billion per year; from 1955 to 1963, the secondary market operations of the Federal National Mortgage Association (FNMA) have added a net of $2.1 billion of assets to the Association's portfolio; during the same nine years, government-sponsored enterprises (for example, Federal Home Loan Banks) have made net loans of more than $4.7 billion. The Case VI and Case VII capital budget models have been designed to supplement the preceding models in this respect.

Case VI: The Inclusion of Nonfederally-Owned Assets

The first alternative—Case VI—is based on a broader definition of government capital investment and on the consolidated cash budget. This model includes additions to capital assets already covered in Case I and federal outlays which result in additions to state, local, and private assets. Through use of the consolidated cash budget, the transactions of trust funds and government-sponsored enterprises—the Federal Land Banks, Federal Home Loan Banks, Federal Intermediate Credit Banks, Banks for Cooperatives, and the Federal Deposit Insurance Corporation—are covered in addition to the transactions recorded in the administrative budget. The Case VI model is a descriptive-type capital budget in the same sense as the Case I model, in that no allowances are made for depreciation or anticipated losses on loans. It also defines national defense outlays as current expenditures.

The transactions of government-sponsored enterprises are shown on a net expenditure basis. The reason for this is that in the consolidated cash budget a measurement of the expenditures of these enterprises is constructed from their net borrowing transactions. In this model the net expenditures of the Federal Deposit Insurance Corporation, mainly claims and expenses minus premium receipts and interest on investments, are classified as current expense. When there is an excess of receipts over expenditures, the result is counted as a negative expenditure. The net expenditures of the Federal Intermediate Credit Banks and the Banks for Cooperatives, both partially owned by the federal government, are classified as federal loans—additions to federal capital assets. On the other hand, the net expenditures of the Federal Land Banks and the Federal Home Loan Banks, which are wholly owned by the participating private members, are classified as additions to private assets.

Cash totals for capital receipts and expenditures are derived after certain adjustments were made to eliminate intragovernmental transactions. These intragovernmental transactions between the budget and trust accounts are receipts of one account and expenditures of another. Since they do not involve a flow of cash to the public they are deducted from the total of budget and trust fund receipts or payments to derive cash receipts from and payments to the public for the capital account. For example, from fiscal year 1955 to 1960 the administrative budget included varying amounts of FNMA loans to the FNMA trust fund. While these amounts are recorded as administrative budget expenditures, on a consolidated cash basis they are simply transactions between government accounts. These expenditures are subtracted from combined capital expenditures to derive cash capital payments to the public. Similarly, loan expenditures from the general fund to the account of the District of Columbia and net advances from the general fund to the unemployment trust fund are also deducted.[1] Likewise, repayments of District of Columbia loans to the general fund are deducted from capital receipts to derive cash capital receipts from the public.

The method and the data employed for the Case VI model are the same as for the Case I model with the exception that the former has adopted a broader concept of capital asset and also includes certain trust fund transactions of a capital nature.[2]

The Federal Contribution to Capital Formation

The principal reason for broadening the scope of the capital asset concept in Case VI is to give a more complete picture of the federal government's gross contribution to capital formation. It is especially important to emphasize the word gross in this context because in the Case VI model no allowance is made for depreciation or related charges. The conceptual problem involved in measuring the federal contribution is the treatment of federal expenditures for additions to state, local and private assets. On the one hand, if these outlays are excluded, the federal government's role in the process of capital formation is grossly understated. Even though the federal government does not acquire a capital asset through its programs of grants-in-aid and subsidies, these expenditures represent a contribution to the nation's total wealth and help to increase the nation's capacity to produce a greater national income in future years. Based on this line of reasoning, the cost of these assets should be included in the federal capital account.

On the other hand, ownership is an inherent part of the generally understood concepts of capital and depreciation accounting.[3]

---

[1] In fiscal year 1963 net repayments to the general fund from the unemployment trust fund are added to the combined total. Only the net of disbursements and repayments is added to or subtracted from the combined total because these unemployment trust fund transactions are recorded on a net basis.

[2] All data are shown in detail in Tables E-1 and E-2 of Appendix E.

[3] In the early capital budgets of the Republic of India, grants to states for developmental purposes were charged to the capital account. In 1951 this practice was reversed because such expenditures did not result in the creation of any permanent assets for the government of India.

TABLE 19. Consolidated Cash Receipts and Payments by Current and Capital Account, Including Additions to State, Local and Private Assets, Fiscal Years 1955–63[a]

(In millions of dollars)

Budget Category	1955	1956	1957	1958	1959	1960	1961	1962	1963
Current account									
Expenditures..........	65,277	67,318	76,304	78,996	82,385	86,137	92,182	97,748	104,186
Receipts..........	67,402	76,526	80,151	79,444	79,043	91,971	93,881	98,501	105,728
Surplus (+) or deficit (−)...........	2,125	9,208	3,847	448	−3,342	5,834	1,699	753	1,542
Capital account[b]									
Expenditures..........	11,958	11,074	9,488	9,114	16,447	13,469	10,852	14,362	16,768
Receipts..........	7,131	6,408	7,740	7,086	6,697	8,385	6,853	7,812	11,214
Surplus (+) or deficit (−)...........	−4,827	−4,666	−1,748	−2,028	−9,750	−5,084	−3,999	−6,550	−5,554
Consolidated cash budget surplus (+) or deficit (−)...........	−2,702	4,542	2,099	−1,580	−13,092	750	−2,300	−5,797	−4,012

[a] Capital expenditures and receipts are gross by the amount of loan repayments (including those repayments going directly into miscellaneous receipts). All national defense outlays are defined as current expenditures.
[b] Source, Appendix E, Table E-2.

From the standpoint of business accounting practices, the cost of these items should be included in the current account if the ownership criterion is not satisfied.

The alternatives are to exclude federal expenditures for additions to state, local and private assets from the capital account and understate the government's contribution to capital formation or to exclude these items from the current account, making an allowance for depreciation, contrary to generally accepted business accounting practice. The Case VI capital budget is a compromise. It excludes expenditures for nonfederally-owned assets from the current account but no allowance is made for the depreciation or obsolescence of any of these assets.

The scope of capital receipts under Case VI assumptions is also broadened to include revenues which are directly related to expenditures for additions to state, local and private assets, and revenues which are earmarked for trust funds engaged in capital type activities. Thus, in addition to the financial receipts included in the Case I capital receipts account and the loan repayments for credit programs in the trust accounts, Case VI capital receipts include the highway trust fund excise taxes and the contributed funds of the Corps of Engineers' civil works trust fund.[4] It does, however, exclude intragovernmental transactions that are included in the Case I capital receipts account.

Budget Surpluses and Deficits

Table 19 shows the results of segregating current and capital cash receipts and payments. The most striking and interesting result is the surplus that occurs in the current account in every year that originally had a deficit in the consolidated cash budget, except for 1959 when the cash budget deficit was $13.1 billion. While there are a few years when this result was produced under Case III, Case IV and Case V assumptions, these changes are the rule rather than the exception in the Case VI model.

One of the most important factors responsible for this result is the broadening of the Case VI concept of capital to include federal expenditures for additions to state, local and private as-

[4] The latter funds consist of contributions by local interests to be used for flood control and river harbor improvement work for the benefit of the contributing localities.

sets. This excludes from the current account a larger amount of expenditures than related receipts. This is particularly true in the later years because grants-in-aid to state and local governments increased noticeably during the nine-year period covered in this study. The current account surplus also partially results from the failure to take an allowance for depreciation and obsolescence which would have increased expenditures in the current account.

The Level of Cash Capital Payments

Table 20 shows that during the period 1955 to 1963 nondefense cash capital payments of the federal government fluctuated from a low of $9.1 billion in 1958 to a high of $16.8 billion in 1963. As a percentage of total nondefense cash payments, capital outlays averaged about 25 percent over the entire period. There are several sharp deviations from this average during the period, however. In 1955, nondefense cash capital payments were

TABLE 20. Nondefense Cash Capital Payments as a Percentage of Total Nondefense Cash Payments, Fiscal Years 1955–63[a]

(Dollar amounts in millions)

Fiscal Year	Adjusted Cash Payments to the Public			Nondefense Cash Capital Payments	
	Total	National Defense	Nondefense	Amount	Percent of Total Nondefense Cash Payments
1955	$ 77,235	$40,852	$36,383	$11,958	32.9%
1956	78,392	40,854	37,538	11,074	29.5
1957	85,792	43,442	42,350	9,488	22.4
1958	88,110	44,552	43,558	9,114	20.9
1959	98,832	46,673	52,159	16,447	31.5
1960	99,606	45,915	53,691	13,469	25.1
1961	103,034	47,685	55,349	10,852	19.6
1962	112,110	51,462	60,648	14,362	23.7
1963	120,954	53,429	67,525	16,768	24.8
1955 to 1963 (weighted average)...................................					25.3

[a] Since cash capital payments are gross of loan repayments, total cash payments and nondefense cash payments are adjusted by a comparable amount. Source, Table 19 and the *Budget of the United States Government, 1965,* Table 19, p. 462.

nearly 33 percent of total nondefense cash outlays. Over the next three years, they fell sharply to a level of about 21 percent when total nondefense cash outlays increased while cash capital payments decreased. In fiscal 1959, however, nondefense cash capital payments rose sharply to about 32 percent of total nondefense cash outlays, only to decline sharply again over the next two years. The ratio then rose to about 24 percent in 1962 and 25 percent in 1963.

The sharp increase in the ratio of cash capital payments to total nondefense cash payments in fiscal 1959 reflects the inclusion in the capital account of administrative budget expenditures for a $1.4 billion nonrecurring subscription to the International Monetary Fund and for the special $1 billion anti-recession emergency housing (mortgage purchase) program enacted by the Congress. The 1959 budget also included a sharp increase in trust fund (including government-sponsored enterprise) capital outlays, including over $1 billion for the interstate highway program and nearly $1.5 billion for Federal Home Loan Bank loans.

Federal vs. Private Capital Investment

A comparison of federal and private investment expenditures gives a rough approximation of the federal government's contribution to capital formation relative to the contribution of the private sector of the economy. Before such a comparison can be made, however, the gross cash capital payments data must be adjusted to exclude financial investment.

Federal expenditures for capital-type goods are not included as a part of gross private fixed investment in the national income accounts. Gross private fixed investment is defined as gross private domestic investment minus the change in business inventories. Thus it includes only investments in physical assets; all financial investments are excluded. The cash payments data developed in Table 19 to show federal nondefense capital outlays must be adjusted, therefore, to delete all financial investments—that is, loans —in order to be comparable with private investment in the national income accounts. The results are shown in Table 21.

As indicated in Table 21, physical nondefense cash capital payments of the federal government appear to be increasing relative to similar expenditures by the private sector of the economy.

TABLE 21. Federal Nondefense Capital Payments to the Public and Gross Private Fixed Investment, Fiscal Years 1955–63[a]

Fiscal Year	Gross Federal Nondefense Capital Payments (Millions of dollars)			Gross Private Fixed Investment (Billions of dollars)	Percent of Total Physical Capital	
	Total	Loans[b]	Physical Capital		Federal	Private
1955	$11,958	$ 8,629	$3,329	$53.4	5.8%	94.2%
1956	11,074	7,620	3,454	61.0	5.4	94.6
1957	9,488	7,455	2,033	64.2	3.0	97.0
1958	9,114	5,629	3,485	61.3	5.4	94.6
1959	16,447	10,817	5,630	62.2	8.3	91.7
1960	13,469	7,242	6,227	67.8	8.4	91.6
1961	10,852	5,077	5,775	66.7	8.0	92.0
1962	14,362	8,897	5,465	70.1	7.3	92.8
1963	16,768	9,257	7,511	75.2	9.1	90.9

[a] Source, U. S. Department of Commerce, Office of Business Economics, *U. S. Income and Output* (1958), p. 121; and *Survey of Current Busines* (July 1964), p. 7; and Joint Economic Committee, *Economic Indicators* (August 1964), p. 8.

[b] This figure is total civil loans including net (loan) expenditures of the Federal Home Loan Banks, Federal Intermediate Credit Banks, Banks for Cooperatives, and the Federal Land Banks.

It is extremely difficult to generalize, however, because of the great degree of instability in the figures for both the government and the private components.

Case VII: Allowances for Depreciation and Related Charges

The seventh and final capital budget model analyzed in this study is also based on the consolidated cash budget. Unlike Case VI, however, this model defines only those nondefense assets that are federally owned as capital, excluding additions to state, local and private assets.[5] Case VII also carries capital budgeting beyond the Case VI model and provides an annual allowance for depreciation and related charges on both new and previously-acquired assets. In this respect, it is similar to the Case II model discussed in an earlier chapter.

[5] In Appendix F, the Case VII current account is adjusted to reflect the exclusion of federal payments for nonfederally-owned assets.

Conceptually, Case VII is a more realistic approach to capital budgeting for the federal government than is Case VI. Although broadening the capital asset concept to include federally-financed but nonfederally-owned assets produces useful economic data, it is difficult to justify the inclusion of nonfederally-owned assets on the government's balance sheet or to include an allowance for depreciation for these assets in a government income statement. If only federally-owned capital assets are included in the capital account, the effect of loan financing, for accounting purposes, is to increase federal debt (liabilities) and federal assets by the same amount, thereby leaving the total net worth of the federal government unchanged. However, if the government borrows funds to finance assets that would belong to a nonfederal entity, the government's net worth would decline since its liabilities would increase while its assets would remain the same. It is true, of course, that the nation's assets would be greater than otherwise, but only a system of national balance sheets[6] would show a private, state or local asset as an offset to the federal financial liability.

Estimating Depreciation and Loss Allowances

Basically, the Case VII model is the same as Case II with the exception that the former is based on the consolidated cash budget, and thus includes the capital expenditures and receipts of certain trust funds, including government-sponsored enterprises, with minor adjustments for intragovernmental transactions, plus the related allowances for depreciation and other charges. The additional data on capital outlays by trust accounts are obtained from annual budget documents (for the early years) and Special Analysis D[7] (for the later years). The estimates of loss allowances on loans made by the Federal Banks for Cooperatives and the Federal National Mortgage Association are made on the basis of loss reserves reported for these agencies in *A Study of Federal Credit Programs.*[8] No loss allowance is computed for Veterans Administration life

---

[6] For a discussion of national balance sheets see Raymond W. Goldsmith and Robert E. Lipsey, *Studies in the National Balance Sheet of the United States,* 2 Volumes (Princeton University Press for National Bureau of Economic Research, 1963).

[7] U.S. Bureau of the Budget, "Investment, Operating and Other Expenditures," *The Budget of the United States Government* (fiscal years 1957-65).

[8] House Subcommittee on Domestic Finance, Committee on Banking and Currency, 88 Cong., 2 sess. (Feb. 28, 1964), pp. 103-108.

TABLE 22. Consolidated Cash Receipts and Payments by Current and Capital Account, Including Depreciation and Related Charges, Fiscal Years 1955–63[a]

(In millions of dollars)

Budget Category	1955	1956	1957	1958	1959	1960	1961	1962	1963
Total current account expenditures......	67,810	70,229	79,387	82,082	88,242	91,971	97,165	104,466	110,453
Expenditures................	66,565	68,937	77,909	80,753	87,013	90,749	95,910	102,831	108,974
Depreciation and related charges[b].	1,245	1,292	1,478	1,329	1,229	1,222	1,255	1,635	1,479
Current receipts................	67,402	76,526	81,630	81,472	81,118	94,510	96,679	101,450	109,007
Surplus (+) or deficit (—)............	−408	6,297	2,243	−610	−7,124	2,539	−486	−3,016	−1,446
Capital account expenditures[c]...........	10,670	9,455	7,883	7,357	11,819	8,857	7,124	9,279	11,980
Total capital receipts.............	8,376	7,700	7,739	6,387	5,851	7,068	5,310	6,498	9,414
Financial receipts[c]...........	7,131	6,408	6,261	5,058	4,622	5,846	4,055	4,863	7,935
Depreciation and related charges[b].	1,245	1,292	1,478	1,329	1,229	1,222	1,255	1,635	1,479
Surplus (+) or deficit (—)............	−2,294	−1,755	−144	−970	−5,968	−1,789	−1,814	−2,781	−2,566
Consolidated cash budget surplus (+) or deficit (—)............	−2,702	4,542	2,099	−1,580	−13,092	750	−2,300	−5,797	−4,012

Note: Detail may not add to totals because of rounding.
[a] Total financial receipts and expenditures are overstated by the amount of loan repayments (excluding those repayments going directly into miscellaneous receipts). All national defense outlays are classified as current expenditures.
[b] Source, Appendix E, Table E-1.
[c] Source, Appendix E, Table E-2.

insurance loans because these loans are completely secured by policy values. Federal Intermediate Credit Banks (FICB) are assumed to have a zero loss ratio. These banks lend only to Production Credit Associations which themselves have had small losses. It seems unlikely that the credit corporations would default to the FICB. No depreciation allowances are estimated for the Corps of Engineers trust fund since the funds contributed by the local communities for capital projects are classified as capital receipts and completely cover the cost of such projects. [9]

Budget Surpluses and Deficits

Table 22 summarizes consolidated cash budget receipts and payments after they have been separated into current and capital accounts and allowances have been made for depreciation and related charges. This table shows the total surplus or deficit on a consolidated cash budget basis compared with the recalculated surplus or deficit in the current and capital accounts.

As in Case VI, which is also based on consolidated cash budget data, the current account deficits in fiscal years 1955, 1958, 1959, 1961, 1962 and 1963 are significantly lower than the consolidated cash budget deficits. Similarly, the current account surpluses in fiscal years 1956 and 1960 are significantly greater than the figures shown for the cash budget, and in fiscal year 1957 the current account surplus is slightly above the cash budget figure. Unlike Case VI, however, in no instance does the separation of receipts and payments into current and capital accounts produce a current account surplus for any year that originally had a cash budget deficit.

In terms of the differences between total budget surpluses and deficits and those of the current accounts of the various models, the results of the Case VII model resemble more closely the results of the Case I and Case II models than those obtained under Case VI assumptions. There is also a close correspondence between the Case VII and the Case V model where an allowance for depreciation and related charges was provided only for assets acquired

---

[9] This is an example where there are two alternative procedures available for recording the cost of the capital project. In addition to the procedure used in this study, all contributed funds could have been classified as current receipts. The cost of the capital project could then have been accounted for by charging an annual depreciation allowance to the current account which would then become a capital receipt.

TABLE 23. Summary of Adjusted Capital Outlays for All Model Capital Budgets and Total Budget Deficits and Surpluses, Fiscal Years 1955–63.ᵃ

(In millions of dollars)

Fiscal Year	Administrative Budget Deficit (−) or Surplus (+)	Case Number				Consolidated Cash Budget Deficit (−) or Surplus (+)	Case Number	
		I & IIᵇ	III	IV	V		VI	VII
1955	−4,180	4,001	13,659	20,335	6,067	−2,702	5,260	3,972
1956	1,626	3,619	12,552	18,662	4,140	4,542	5,228	3,609
1957	1,596	1,833	11,146	18,199	2,166	2,099	3,702	2,097
1958	−2,819	3,002	13,222	20,190	3,394	−1,580	4,476	2,719
1959	−12,427	7,493	16,454	22,506	7,596	−13,092	12,367	7,739
1960	−1,224	3,440	11,594	17,906	3,858	750	8,191	3,579
1961	−3,856	3,542	11,510	18,572	3,649	−2,300	7,360	3,632
1962	−6,378	4,317	12,485	20,404	4,731	−5,797	9,914	4,831
1963	−6,266	5,063	13,467	21,676	5,240	−4,012	9,565	4,777
Total 1955–63	−31,480	36,010	116,089	178,450	40,841	−22,092	66,063	36,955

ᵃ Source, Table 1, Table 11, Table 14, Table 15, Table 16, Table 22, Table E-2. In all cases, capital outlays are net of loan repayments.
ᵇ Net capital outlays are the same for both cases.

since 1955. There is a sharp difference between the results obtained in Case VII and Case IV, but the most noticeable difference in results is between Case VII and Case VI which is also based on the consolidated cash budget. These differences reflect two factors. First, Cases IV and VI are based on a broader concept of capital assets. In Case VI, expenditures for additions to state, local and private assets were excluded from the current account and classified as federal capital outlays; in Case IV all military assets were considered capital assets. Secondly, Case VI failed to take an allowance for depreciation on assets or losses on loans classified as capital assets.

The Level of Capital Outlays

In Table 23, capital payments minus loan repayments[10] are compared with budget surpluses and deficits. For Case VII, in four of the six years when there was a consolidated cash deficit, gross nondefense cash capital payments minus loan repayments are considerably more than the amount of the cash deficit. Only in 1959, when the cash deficit was quite large, $13.1 billion, and in 1962 does the deficit exceed cash capital outlays. Cumulated for the entire nine-year period, cash outlays for federally-owned capital and financial assets exceed the net cash deficit by nearly $15 billion.

This does not mean, however, that net additions to the federal government's stock of nondefense capital assets have been continually greater than the cumulative net cash budget deficits during this period. To make such a judgment, it is necessary to make an additional adjustment of cash capital payments for such factors as depreciation, obsolescence and sales of assets. When these adjustments are made, net nondefense cash capital payments during the period 1955 to 1963 are $20.1 billion as compared to a net cash deficit of $22.1 billion, or $2.0 billion less. Even on this basis, however, the ratio of net nondefense cash capital payments to the net cash deficit is quite impressive for the period as a whole.

[10] One item included in gross capital payments is short-term loans, in many cases, such as Commodity Credit Corporation and Housing and Home Finance Agency loans, loans of much less than a year. Because they have such short maturities, many of these loans may not be reflected in the cash deficit even though they are a part of gross capital expenditures. Therefore, in order to make a meaningful comparison, cash capital payments should be net of loan repayments.

This relationship of capital outlays to budget deficits also occurs in each of the preceding capital budget models. In fact, it is even more positive for the Case III and Case IV models where defense as well as nondefense expenditures are excluded from the current account. Thus, as a general conclusion, it can be said that during the period fiscal years 1955 to 1963 federal outlays for capital assets which would either be repaid or yield substantial benefits and services in the future exceed significantly the budget deficits incurred.

Nondefense Federally-Owned Capital Assets

THE FOLLOWING TABLES present detailed data for fiscal years 1955 to 1963 on the value of nondefense, federally-owned capital assets and estimated annual depreciation charges or loss allowances on these assets. Case studies I and II, described in Chapters 4 and 5 of the text, are based solely on these data. Cases III, IV, VI and VII are also based on these tables with addition of data on national defense assets (Cases III and IV) and trust fund assets (Cases VI and VII). The source of all depreciation rates used to estimate depreciation charges on this group of capital assets is the staff paper prepared for the Bureau of the Budget by Robert Hubbell and Wilfred Lewis, Jr., "Estimates of Depreciation, Obsolescence, and Losses on Federal Assets in the Fiscal Years 1955 and 1956" (July 1957).

TABLE A-1. Federal Buildings

(In millions of dollars)

Fiscal Year	Value of Assets, End of Year[a]	Estimated Depreciation Charge[b]
1955	3,988	83
1956	4,031	84
1957	3,946	82
1958	4,001	84
1959	4,172	87
1960	4,406	92
1961	4,764	100
1962	5,066	106
1963	5,372	112

[a] Data on asset values are from General Services Administration, *Inventory Report on Real Property Owned by the U.S. Throughout the World* (fiscal years 1955–63), Table 2. Data include the value of the buildings of the Architect of the Capitol and leasehold improvements not included in the inventory report totals.

[b] The estimated depreciation rate used is 2.09 percent.

113

TABLE A-2. Structures and Facilities

(In millions of dollars)

Fiscal Year	Value of Assets, End of Year[a]	Estimated Depreciation Charge[b]
1955	8,558	141
1956	9,038	149
1957	9,591	158
1958	10,011	165
1959	10,463	173
1960	11,297	186
1961	12,013	198
1962	13,093	216
1963	13,772	227

[a] Data on asset values are from General Services Administration *Inventory Report on Real Property Owned by the U.S. Throughout the World,* (fiscal years 1955–63), Table 2.
[b] The estimated depreciation rate used is 1.65 percent.

TABLE A-3. Machinery and Equipment

(In millions of dollars)

Fiscal Year	Value of Assets, End of Year[a]				Estimated Depreciation Charge[b]			
	Total	Maritime	Treasury	Other	Total	Maritime	Treasury	Other
1955	7,485	4,680	551	2,254	372	234	22	116
1956	7,374	4,484	549	2,341	367	224	22	121
1957	7,338	4,338	530	2,470	365	217	21	127
1958	7,444	4,455	541	2,448	371	223	22	126
1959	7,717	4,571	536	2,610	385	229	21	135
1960	7,893	4,408	550	2,935	393	220	22	151
1961	8,382	4,388	547	3,447	419	219	22	178
1962	8,381	4,146	560	3,675	419	207	22	190
1963	8,988	4,339	580	4,069	450	217	23	210

[a] Data on asset values are from the *Federal Real and Personal Property Inventory Report (Civilian and Military) of the United States Government Covering Its Properties Located in the United States, in the Territories, and Overseas,* House Committee on Government Operations (fiscal years 1955–63).
[b] The estimated depreciation rates used are 5 percent on maritime, 4 percent on Treasury (Coast Guard) and 5.16 percent on other assets.

TABLE A-4. Libraries

(In millions of dollars)

Fiscal Year	Value of Assets, End of Year[a]	Estimated Depreciation Charge[b]
1955	2,306	76
1956	2,312	76
1957	2,315	76
1958	2,331	77
1959	2,352	78
1960	2,366	78
1961	2,380	79
1962	2,385	79
1963	2,389	79

[a] Data on asset values are from the *Federal Real and Personal Property Inventory Report (Civilian and Military)* of the *United States Government Covering Its Properties Located in the United States, in the Territories, and Overseas,* House Committee on Government Operations (fiscal years 1955–63). This category includes primarily books at the Library of Congress and is listed under Library of Congress in the above source.
[b] The estimated depreciation rate used is 3.3 percent.

TABLE A-5. Estimated Losses on Loans[a]

(Dollar amounts in millions)

Agency or Program[b]	1955	1956	1957	1958	1959	1960	1961	1962	1963	Loss Rate (Percent)
Housing and Home Finance Agency:										
Federal National Mortgage Association	$ 0.5	$ 0.4	$ 1.0	$ 0.8	$ 1.4	$ 1.4	$ 0.2	$ 0.2	$ 0.1	.10%
Urban Renewal Administration	*	*	*	*	*	*	*	*	*	.01
Community Facilities Administration	.1	.1	.2	.4	.5	.6	.6	.7	.9	.25
Federal Housing Administration	19.6	17.2	14.4	13.3	12.8	20.3	31.5	22.4	36.3	a
Public Housing Administration	.3	.4	.4	.3	.2	.2	.2	.3	.6	.15
Veterans Administration	.1	.2	.2	.4	.5	.6	.5	.6	.8	a
Department of Agriculture:										
Rural Electrification Administration	*	*	*	*	*	*	*	*	*	.01
Farmers Home Administration	4.7	4.9	6.2	6.7	7.0	6.2	7.4	11.7	15.2	2.00
Department of Commerce:										
Area Redevelopment Administration	—	—	—	—	—	—	—	*	.5	2.00
Maritime Administration	—	—	—	*	*	—	*	—	*	.20
Small Business Administration	.6	1.5	2.4	3.2	4.4	3.6	4.8	8.7	7.3	2.50
Department of Health, Education, and Welfare	—	—	—	—	.2	.3	.4	.6	.7	.75
Export-Import Bank	.5	.5	.6	2.1	1.9	1.1	1.3	2.3	1.3	.25
Agency for International Development	3.0	3.3	3.6	7.4	11.9	10.1	14.7	20.7	28.8	2.00
Other agencies or programs	.7	.3	—	—	10.1	—	.4	1.5	—	.75
Total estimated loss allowance	30.1	28.8	29.0	34.6	50.9	44.4	62.0	69.7	92.5	

* Less than $500 thousand.

a The estimates for loss allowances on loans are obtained by applying a percentage loss rate to the dollar amount of annual disbursements for each loan program. Except for Veterans Administration and Federal Housing Administration loans, disbursement data are from U.S. Bureau of the Budget, Special Analysis E, "Federal Credit Programs," The Budget of the United States Government (fiscal years 1957–65); loss rate percentages are computed on the basis of data submitted by the various federal credit agencies in response to a questionnaire sent by the House Subcommittee on Domestic Finance, Committee on Banking and Currency. The amount of VA loans established and FHA loans acquired, and estimated losses for both agencies are based on financial statements for these agencies.

b There is no loss allowance for Commodity Credit Corporation loans because the realized annual loss estimated for this program is relatively small and, in this study, is included in the CCC loss allowance for major commodity inventories. Federal Intermediate Credit Banks have had a 100 percent recovery record and therefore no loss allowance is estimated. There is also no estimated loss allowance for the United Kingdom loan since it is expected that repayment will be made in full (i.e., an implicit zero loss allowance).

TABLE A-6. Estimated Losses on Acquired Property: Federal Housing Administration and Veterans Administration[a]

(In millions of dollars)

Fiscal Year	FHA Gross Acquisitions of Real Properties	Estimated Loss on FHA Acquired Property	Actual Veterans Administration Loss on Acquired Property	Total Estimated Loss on Acquired Property
1955	39	6	*	6
1956	68	10	1	11
1957	43	6	2	8
1958	30	4	3	7
1959	36	5	5	10
1960	56	8	5	13
1961	159	24	8	32
1962	310	47	13	60
1963	426	64	16	80

* Less than $500 thousand.

[a] The estimated loss on FHA acquired property is obtained by applying a percentage loss rate (15 percent) to the amount of FHA outlays for acquired property. Data on FHA gross acquisitions of real properties are from U.S. Bureau of the Budget, *The Budget of the United States Government* (fiscal years 1957–1965). The FHA loss rate is based on agency financial statements. The amount of actual VA losses on acquired property is also obtained from agency financial statements.

TABLE A-7. Major Commodity Inventories: Commodity Credit Corporation[a]

(In millions of dollars)

Fiscal Year	Program Losses	Minus Expenses for Storage, Handling and Transportation	Estimated Loss Allowance
1955	904	374	531
1956	1,067	499	568
1957	1,252	503	749
1958	1,087	508	579
1959	973	539	434
1960	963	559	404
1961	946	591	355
1962	1,210	527	683
1963	985	547	438

Note: Detail may not add to totals because of rounding.

[a] Data on program losses and expenses for storage, handling and transportation are from the U.S. Department of Agriculture and are consistent with budget data shown in the U.S. budget document. The data on program losses include a small amount of losses on Commodity Credit Corporation loans not separately identifiable.

117

TABLE A-8. Major Commodity Inventories: Emergency Civil Defense Supplies

(In millions of dollars)

Fiscal Year[a]	Value of Inventory, End of Year[b]	Estimated Loss Allowance[c]
1955	106	5
1956	139	7
1957	174	9
1958	207	10
1959	198	10
1960	209	10
1961	188	9

[a] Data for fiscal year 1961 are obtained directly from the Department of Health, Education, and Welfare. Starting with fiscal year 1962, emergency supplies are classified as national defense; therefore, loss allowances for fiscal years 1962 and 1963 are shown in Appendix B, Table B-5.

[b] Data on the inventory evaluation are from *Federal Real and Personal Property Inventory Report (Civilian and Military) of the United States Government Covering Its Properties Located in the United States, in the Territories, and Overseas,* House Committee on Government Operations (fiscal years 1955–1960).

[c] The estimated annual loss rate used is 5 percent and is taken from Hubbell and Lewis, op. cit.

Defense Capital Assets: The Narrow Definition

THE FOLLOWING TABLES present detailed data for fiscal years 1955 to 1963 on the value of defense assets and depreciation and related charges on them as these assets are defined for purposes of Case study III described in Chapter 6 of the text. The depreciation rates used to estimate depreciation charges on this group of assets are primarily from Hubbell and Lewis, "Estimates of Depreciation, Obsolescence, and Losses on Federal Assets in the Fiscal Years 1955 and 1956" (staff paper prepared for the Bureau of the Budget, July 1957).

TABLE B-1. Military Buildings and Structures

(In millions of dollars)

Fiscal Year	Value of Buildings and Structures, End of Year[a]	Estimated Depreciation Charge[b]
1955	20,499	584
1956	22,046	628
1957	24,105	687
1958	26,175	746
1959	28,984	826
1960	31,228	890
1961	33,287	949
1962	34,513	984
1963	35,620	1,015

[a] Data on asset values are from General Services Administration, *Inventory Report on Real Property Owned by the United States in United States Territories and Possessions and in Foreign Countries as of June 30, 1955,* and General Services Administration, *Inventory Report on Real Property Owned by the United States Throughout the World* (fiscal years 1956–1963).
[b] The estimated depreciation rate used is 2.85 percent.

TABLE B-2. Major Military Equipment: Aircraft

(In millions of dollars)

| Fiscal Year | Value of Assets, End of Year[a] | | | | Estimated Depreciation Charge[d] |
	Total	Air Force[b]	Navy	Army[c]	
1955	17,816	13,100	4,600	116	1,619
1956	22,766	17,600	5,000	166	2,069
1957	24,653	19,100	5,300	253	2,241
1958	27,545	21,200	5,900	445	2,504
1959	28,833	22,300	6,100	433	2,621
1960	30,748	24,000	6,100	648	2,795
1961	30,518	23,400	6,400	718	2,774
1962	33,568	24,900	7,900	768	3,051
1963	35,174	25,400	9,000	774	3,197

[a] Data on asset values are from the *Federal Real and Personal Property Inventory Report (Civilian and Military)* of the United States Government Covering Its Properties Located in the United States, in the Territories, and Overseas, House Committee on Government Operations (fiscal years 1955–1963).

[b] Values reported in inventory reports are adjusted to remove amounts for missiles included in inventory values

[c] This detail is not reported separately in the inventory reports and is obtained from the Department of Defense

[d] The estimated depreciation rate used is 9.09 percent.

TABLE B-3. Major Military Equipment: Naval Ships and Craft

(In millions of dollars)

| Fiscal Year | Value of Assets, End of Year[a] | | Estimated Depreciation Charge[b] | | |
	Naval Ships	Naval Craft	Total	Naval Ships	Naval Craft
1955	18,400	924	1,319	1,227	92
1956	19,800	1,000	1,421	1,321	100
1957	20,500	1,000	1,467	1,367	100
1958	21,800	1,000	1,554	1,454	100
1959	21,500	969	1,531	1,434	97
1960	22,100	964	1,570	1,474	96
1961	22,600	930	1,600	1,507	93
1962	23,300	889	1,643	1,554	89
1963	24,500	876	1,722	1,634	88

[a] Data on asset values are from the *Federal Real and Personal Property Inventory Report (Civilian and Military)* of the United States Covering Its Properties Located in the United States, in the Territories, and Overseas, House Committee on Government Operations (fiscal years 1955–1963).

[b] The estimated depreciation rates used are 6.67 percent for naval ships and 10 percent for naval craft.

TABLE B-4. Major Commodity Inventories: Expansion of Defense Production, Metals and Materials

(In millions of dollars)

Fiscal Year	Value of Acquisitions[a]	Estimated Loss Allowance[b]
1955	483	53
1956	265	29
1957	217	24
1958	495	54
1959	247	27
1960	135	15
1961	72	8
1962	57	6
1963	21	2

[a] Data are for the gross acquisitions of the program. Figures are from U.S. Bureau of the Budget, *The Budget of the United States Government* (fiscal years 1957–65).
[b] The estimated rate of loss used is 11 percent of the value of each year's yearly gross acquisitions and is based on the (unweighted) average ratio of actual losses from sales to gross sales.

TABLE B-5. Major Commodity Inventories: Emergency Civil Defense Supplies

(In millions of dollars)

Fiscal Year	Value of Inventory, End of Year[a]	Estimated Loss Allowance[b]
1962	194	10
1963	224	11

[a] Data are from the Department of Defense. Data for the years 1955–1961, when emergency supplies were not classified as national defense, are shown in Appendix A, Table A-8.
[b] The estimated annual loss rate used is 5 percent and is taken from Hubbell and Lewis ,op. cit

TABLE B-6. National Defense Loans: Expansion of Defense Production

(In millions of dollars)

Fiscal Year	Disbursements[a]	Estimated Loss Allowance[b]
1955	81	8
1956	61	6
1957	29	3
1958	49	5
1959	30	3
1960	26	3
1961	17	2
1962	24	2
1963	15	2

[a] Data on the amount of gross disbursements are from U.S. Bureau of the Budget, Special Analysis E, "Federal Credit Programs," *The Budget of the United States Government* (fiscal years 1957–65).
[b] The estimated annual loss rate used is 10 percent and is taken from Hubbell and Lewis, *op. cit.*

TABLE B-7. Major Commodity Inventories: Stockpile of Strategic and Critical Materials[a]

(In millions of dollars)

Fiscal Year	Estimated Loss Allowance
1955	9
1956	7
1957	9
1958	4
1959	10
1960	3[b]
1961	1
1962	3
1963	0

[a] Data are from U.S. Bureau of the Budget, *The Budget of the United States Government* (fiscal years 1957–65). The loss estimate is the actual cost of rotating the inventory. A rotation procedure is used to keep the inventory in usable condition. Since the inventory is not for resale, the cost of rotation approximates the annual cost of the program.
[b] The 1962 U.S. Budget, p. 278, shows $69,376 thousand of rotation sales, but only $11,660 thousand of this was for rotation while the remainder was for the purpose of reducing the inventory. Replacement costs of the materials rotated were $14,395 thousand, yielding a net rotation cost of $2,735 thousand.

Additional Defense Capital Assets

THIS TABLE PRESENTS detailed data for the fiscal years 1955 to 1963 on the additional defense assets that are included in the broader definition of capital upon which Case IV is based. The depreciation rates used to estimate depreciation charges are primarily from Hubbell and Lewis, "Estimates of Depreciation, Obsolescence, and Losses on Federal Assets in the Fiscal Years 1955 and 1956" (staff paper prepared for the Bureau of the Budget, July 1957).

TABLE C-1. Major Military Equipment: Broad Concept

(In millions of dollars)

Fiscal Year	Value of Assets, End of Year[a]			Estimated Depreciation Charge			
	Plant Equipment Inventory	Weapons	Supply Inventories	Total	Plant Equipment Inventory[b]	Weapons[c]	Supply Inventories[d]
1955	5,300	53,300	39,477	9,482	239	4,664	4,579
1956	5,307	55,500	39,772	9,709	239	4,856	4,614
1957	5,300	57,600	42,244	10,179	239	5,040	4,900
1958	5,509	62,100	39,989	10,321	248	5,434	4,639
1959	5,278	63,600	37,513	10,155	238	5,565	4,352
1960	5,233	68,100	35,432	10,304	235	5,959	4,110
1961	5,707	69,500	32,660	10,127	257	6,081	3,789
1962	6,397	75,700	32,658	10,700	288	6,224	3,788
1963	6,663	79,300	30,245	10747	300	6,939	3,508

[a] Data on asset values are obtained from the *Federal Real and Personal Property Inventory Report (Civilian and Military) of the United States Government Covering Its Properties Located in the United States, in the Territories, and Overseas,* House Committee on Government Operations (fiscal years 1955–63).
[b] Assumes an annual depreciation rate of 4.5 percent.
[c] Assumes an annual depreciation rate of 8.75 percent.
[d] Assumes an annual depreciation rate of 11.6 percent.

123

Nondefense, Federally-Owned Capital Assets Acquired Since 1955

THE FOLLOWING TABLES present detailed data for fiscal years 1955 to 1963 on the value of nondefense, federally-owned capital assets acquired only since 1955, estimated annual depreciation charges or loss allowances on these assets, and the estimated repayment schedule of federal loans made since 1955. The asset categories (public works, major equipment, other physical assets, and so forth) are those used in U.S. Bureau of Budget, Special Analysis D, "Investment, Operating and Other Expenditures." Case Study V, described in Chapter 7 of the text, is based on these data with the addition of the data on estimated losses on loans from Table A-5, Appendix A. The depreciation rates used to estimate depreciation allowances and related charges are from Hubbell and Lewis, "Estimates of Depreciation, Obsolescence, and Losses on Federal Assets in the Fiscal Years 1955 and 1956" (staff paper prepared for the Bureau of the Budget, July 1957) and from U.S. Bureau of the Budget, *The Budget of the United States Government*.

TABLE D-1. Public Works

(In millions of dollars)

Fiscal Year	Expenditures[a]	Cumulative Expenditures	Estimated Depreciation Charge[b]
1955	1,024	1,024	18
1956	867	1,891	34
1957	1,075	2,966	53
1958	1,252	4,218	76
1959	1,506	5,724	103
1960	1,633	7,357	132
1961	1,874	9,231	166
1962	2,046	11,277	203
1963	2,289	13,566	244

[a] Data on public works expenditures are from U.S. Bureau of the Budget, Special Analysis D, "Investment, Operating and Other Expenditures" (fiscal years 1957–65).
[b] The estimated depreciation rate used is 1.8 percent.

TABLE D-2. Major Equipment: Ships

(In millions of dollars)

Fiscal Year	Commerce Department: Ships		Estimated Depreciation Charge[b]
	Annual Expenditures[a]	Cumulative Expenditures	
1955	24	24	1
1956	14	38	2
1957	14	52	3
1958	11	63	3
1959	22	85	4
1960	27	112	6
1961	15	127	6
1962	20	147	7
1963	17	164	8

[a] Data on annual expenditures are from U.S. Bureau of the Budget, Special Analysis D, "Investment, Operating and Other Expenditures" (fiscal years 1957–65). The assets are ships acquired by the Maritime Administration.
[b] The estimated depreciation rate used is 5 percent.

TABLE D-3. Other Equipment

(In millions of dollars)

Fiscal Year	Annual Expenditures[a]	Cumulative Expenditures	Estimated Depreciation Charge[b]
1955	24	24	1
1956	6	30	2
1957	18	48	2
1958	28	76	4
1959	39	115	6
1960	53	168	9
1961	36	204	11
1962	100	304	16
1963	105	409	21

[a] Data on annual expenditures are from U.S. Bureau of the Budget, Special Analysis D, "Investment, Operating and Other Expenditures" (fiscal years 1957–65). The assets are primarily held by the Treasury Department (including some for Coast Guard ship construction which are not separately identifiable), the Post Office, NASA, Federal Aviation Administration and the Library of Congress.

[b] The estimated depreciation rate used is 5.16 percent.

TABLE D-4. Other Physical Assets

(In millions of dollars)

Fiscal Year	Annual Expenditures[a]	Cumulative Expenditures	Estimated Depreciation Charge[b]
1955	13	13	*
1956	18	31	1
1957	19	50	1
1958	27	77	2
1959	44	121	2
1960	30	151	3
1961	109	260	5
1962	47	307	6
1963	65	372	7

* Less than $500,000.

[a] Data on annual expenditures are from U.S. Bureau of the Budget, Special Analysis D, "Investment, Operating and Other Expenditures" (fiscal years 1957–65). The assets are primarily those owned by the Department of Agriculture and the Department of Interior.

[b] The depreciation rate used is 2 percent.

TABLE D-5. Major Commodity Inventories: Commodity Credit Corporation[a]

(Dollar amounts in millions)

Fiscal Year	Commodity Inventory, Beginning Of Fiscal Year	Reported Annual Loss Allowance		Annual Inventory Acquisitions	Estimated Loss Allowance
		Amount	Percent of Inventory		
1955	$4,989	$531	10.6%	$3,435	$364
1956	5,983	568	9.5	3,741	355
1957	5,372	749	13.9	3,715	516
1958	3,310	579	17.5	3,685	645
1959	3,614	434	12.0	3,356	403
1960	4,228	404	9.6	4,621	444
1961	5,565	355	6.4	3,673	235
1962	4,475	683	15.3	2,151	329
1963	4,726	438	9.3	2,868	267

[a] Data on reported annual loss allowances, commodity inventory on hand at the start of the fiscal year, and annual inventory acquisitions are from the U.S. Bureau of the Budget, *The Budget of the United States Government* (fiscal years 1957–65).

TABLE D-6. Major Commodity Inventories: Emergency Civil Defense Supplies

(In millions of dollars)

Fiscal Year	Annual Disbursements[a]	Estimated Loss Allowance[b]
1955	22	1
1956	32	2
1957	33	2
1958	32	2
1959	10	1
1960	9	*
1961	c	c
1962	c	c
1963	c	c

* Less than $500 thousand.
[a] Data on the amount of annual disbursements are from U.S. Bureau of the Budget, *The Budget of the United States Government* (fiscal years 1957–65).
[b] The estimated annual loss rate used is 5 percent.
[c] Prior to 1961 emergency supplies are classified as nondefense items. Since 1961 they have been classified as national defense.

TABLE D-7. Estimated Repayment Schedule of Loans Made Since Fiscal Year 1955[a]

(In millions of dollars)

Agency or Program	1955	1956	1957	1958	1959	1960	1961	1962	1963	Amount of Loans Outstanding at End of Fiscal Year 1954
Housing and Home Finance Agency:										
Federal National Mortgage Association	8	201	974	724	296	889	100	143	437	2,301
Urban Renewal Administration	—	10	23	19	67	124	104	93	156	32
Community Facilities Administration	—	—	—	—	—	—	—	11	28	49
Federal Housing Administration	1	1	2	2	3	4	5	8	103	166
Public Housing Administration	115	239	246	208	151	129	127	172	382	198
Veterans Administration	2	3	5	9	13	19	25	115	576	348
Department of Agriculture:										
Commodity Credit Corporation	3,302	2,754	2,609	2,449	2,659	2,638	1,637	1,916	2,704	360
Rural Electrification Administration	16	22	27	41	46	49	52	77	103	2,164
Farmers Home Administration	29	60	99	140	270	231	262	373	495	647
Federal Intermediate Credit Banks	1,065	1,923	1,229	—	—	—	—	—	—	—
Department of Commerce:										
Area Redevelopment Administration	—	—	—	—	—	—	—	*	*	—
Maritime Administration	—	—	—	—	26	26	27	22	—15	—
Small Business Administration	5	11	94	41	68	87	103	130	166	2
Department of Health, Education, and Welfare	—	—	—	—	—	—	—	*	1	—
Export-Import Bank	13	26	41	96	148	177	213	356	780	2,672
Foreign assistance loans	—	—	—	4	9	22	31	46	56	1,561
District of Columbia	—	—	—	—	—	—	—	8	3	—
Total	4,556	5,250	5,349	3,733	3,756	4,395	2,686	3,470	6,005	

* Less than $500 thousand.

[a] Figures are based on data from U.S. Bureau of the Budget, Special Analysis E, "Federal Credit Programs," The Budget of the United States Government (fiscal years 1957–65).

128

The Consolidated Cash Budget

THE FOLLOWING TABLES present detailed data on capital receipts and payments based on the consolidated cash budget for fiscal years 1955 to 1963. Cases VI and VII described in Chapter 8 of the text are based upon these data.

TABLE E-1. Estimated Depreciation and Related Charges: Consolidated Cash Budget Basis

(In millions of dollars)

Fiscal Year	Estimated Depreciation or Loss Allowance			
	Total	Administrative Budget[a]	FNMA Secondary Market Loans[b]	Banks for Cooperatives Loans[b]
1955	1,245	1,244	*	1
1956	1,292	1,291	*	1
1957	1,478	1,476	1	1
1958	1,329	1,328	1	1
1959	1,229	1,228	*	1
1960	1,222	1,220	1	1
1961	1,255	1,254	1	1
1962	1,635	1,633	1	1
1963	1,479	1,478	*	1

Note: Detail may not add to totals because of rounding.
* Less than $500 thousand.
[a] Source, Table 7, Chapter V.
[b] Assumes a loss rate of .10 percent based on data submitted to the House Subcommittee on Domestic Finance, Committee on Banking and Currency.

TABLE E-2. Derivation of Consolidated Cash Capital Payments and Receipts[a]

(In millions of dollars)

Item	1955	1956	1957	1958	1959	1960	1961	1962	1963
Expenditures									
Administrative budget	10,623	9,390	7,515	7,127	11,352	8,253	6,335	8,201	11,245
Trust funds	140	353	1,295	936	776	1,400	861	1,157	686
Less: Loans to									
FNMA secondary market trust fund	93	286	923	703	307	795	—	—	—
District of Columbia	—	2	4	3	2	1	23	48	36
Unemployment trust fund[b]	—	—	—	—	—	—	49	31	−85
Cash capital payments, excluding additions to state, local and private assets	10,670	9,455	7,883	7,357	11,819	8,857	7,124	9,279	11,980
Plus: Additions to state, local and private assets									
Administrative budget	1,098	1,221	543	790	925	1,134	1,247	1,305	1,312
Trust funds	197	405	1,071	978	3,707	3,480	2,483	3,783	3,481
Less: Grants-in-aid to the District of Columbia	7	7	9	11	4	2	2	5	5
Total cash capital payments, including additions to state, local and private assets	11,958	11,074	9,488	9,114	16,447	13,469	10,852	14,362	16,768
Receipts									
Administrative budget	7,048	6,316	6,146	4,535	4,389	5,669	3,346	4,292	6,890
Trust fund[c]	83	92	115	523	233	177	712	579	1,048
Less: Repayments of District of Columbia loans	—	—	—	—	—	—	3	8	3
Cash capital receipts, excluding additions to state, local and private assets	7,131	6,408	6,261	5,058	4,622	5,846	4,055	4,863	7,935
Plus: Highway excise taxes	—	—	1,479	2,028	2,075	2,539	2,798	2,949	3,279
Total cash capital receipts, including state, local and private assets	7,131	6,408	7,740	7,086	6,697	8,385	6,853	7,812	11,214

[a] Source, Tables 1 and 6; U.S. Bureau of the Budget, *The Budget of the United States Government* (fiscal years 1957–65); and *Supporting Tables of Receipts and Payments to the Public* (fiscal years 1957–65).
[b] Figures are net of repayments.
[c] Consists of repayments of veterans, FNMA and State Rural Rehabilitation Fund loans, and contributed funds of the Corps of Engineers Civil Trust Fund.

130

Inclusion of Nonfederally-Owned Capital Assets in the Capital Account: Case II, Case V and Case VII

THE PURPOSE OF this appendix is to show what the current accounts of three of the models examined in this study—Case II, Case V and Case VII—would look like if they were adjusted to exclude federal expenditures for additions to state, local and private assets.

TABLE F-1. Federal Expenditures for Additions to State, Local and Private Assets, by Type, Fiscal Years 1936–63[a]

(In millions of dollars)

Fiscal Year	Highways[b]	Ships	Hospitals	Schools	Airports	Conservation Facilities and Practices	Waste Treatment and All Other	Total All Assets
1936 to 1954	5,146	455	504	297	175	2,914	310	9,801
1955	585	5	74	121	8	301	4	1,098
1956	729	14	54	89	17	293	25	1,221
1957	2	17	61	67	21	341	34	543
1958	25	28	105	74	43	437	78	790
1959	25	28	135	66	57	528	86	925
1960	29	70	143	71	57	684	75	1,129
1961	32	97	157	59	65	752	85	1,247
1962	31	143	163	42	58	758	111	1,306
1963	39	103	182	53	51	701	183	1,312

[a] Source, U.S. Bureau of the Budget, Special Analysis D (1949 to 1963); *The Budget of the United States Government* (1938 to 1949); Advisory Commission on Intergovernmental Relations, *Periodic Congressional Reassessment of Federal Grants-in-aid to State and Local Governments* (Washington: June 1961).

[b] Beginning with 1957, the highway program was made a trust fund account. These figures are exclusive of trust fund expenditures.

131

Table F-1 presents data for additions to state, local and private assets. These data are obtained from three sources (1) Special Analysis D[1] for the years 1949 to 1963; (2) individual budget documents for the years prior to 1949; and (3) a report of the Advisory Commission on Intergovernmental Relations.[2] The specific types of assets involved are primarily highways, hospitals, merchant ships, various agricultural conservation facilities and practices, schools, airport facilities and waste treatment projects. Since it is not possible to identify the end product of specific expenditures, no adjustments are made to exclude nonphysical assets where they might be classified in Special Analysis D with additions to physical assets. This is particularly true for conservation expenditures which include a mixture of physical assets, such as ponds, terraces, and cover crops, and of payments for taking land out of production.

Although there were sizable federal expenditures for highway construction and conservation facilities and practices prior to 1945, the greater part of federal expenditures for these and other nonfederally-owned assets was made after World War II. For a few of the early years, it was necessary to estimate federal expenditures for private conservation facilities and practices.

The most difficult problem in adjusting for nonfederally-owned assets is compiling an inventory of property for depreciation purposes. There are no records that show what proportion of total state, local and private assets has been financed by the federal government. Consequently, the closest approximation that can be made is to cumulate the annual expenditures by the federal government for the types of assets identified. Although this is a minor problem for the years when Special Analysis D is available, prior to 1949 only fragmentary data are available for certain asset categories. However, relatively good data are available for federal aid for state and local highway construction, and this represents the predominant nonfederally-owned physical assets financed by the federal government during this period.

In Table F-2, federal expenditures from 1936 through 1955 for nonfederally-owned assets are cumulated to derive an estimated inventory (depreciation) base for 1955. In order to compile the depreciation base for each succeeding year, a 20-year moving total is obtained by

---

[1] U.S. Bureau of the Budget, "Investment, Operating and Other Expenditures," *The Budget of the United States Government.* Further references to Special Analysis D refer to this document.

[2] Advisory Commission on Intergovernmental Relations, *Periodic Congressional Reassessment of Federal Grants-In-Aid to State and Local Governments* (Washington: June 1961).

TABLE F-2. Estimated Depreciation Allowances for Federal Expenditures for Additions to State, Local and Private Assets, Fiscal Years 1936–63[a]

(In millions of dollars)

Fiscal Year	Cumulative Expenditures, 1955 and After		20-Year Moving Expenditure Total	
	Amount	Estimated Depreciation Allowance[b]	Amount	Estimated Depreciation Allowance[b]
1936 to 1954			9,801	
1955	1,098	55	10,899	545
1956	2,319	116	11,875	594
1957	2,862	143	12,056	603
1958	3,652	183	12,599	630
1959	4,577	229	13,272	664
1960	5,706	285	13,971	699
1961	6,953	348	14,881	744
1962	8,259	413	15,858	793
1963	9,571	479	16,873	844

[a] Source, Table F-1.
[b] The rate of depreciation used is 5 per cent.

adding to the 1955 base figure the expenditures for one additional year and subtracting the expenditures for one earlier year. For example, the depreciation base for 1956 includes expenditures for the 20-year period 1937 through 1956; for 1957 the base includes expenditures for the period 1938 through 1957, and so forth.

A depreciation rate of five percent is used to calculate depreciation charges assuming an average useful life of 20 years for these assets. It is assumed that highways have a useful life of 25 years; schools, 33⅓ years; hospitals, 50 years; ships, 20 years; airports, 40 years; conservation facilities and practices, 15 years; and waste treatment facilities, 66 years.[3] By weighting each type of expenditure by the appropriate estimated useful life (or depreciation rate) it was possible to compile a rough estimate of the average useful life (or average depreciation rate) for all federally-financed but nonfederally-owned assets.

[3] Based on Hubbell and Lewis, "Estimates of Depreciation, Obsolescence, and Losses on Federal Assets in the Fiscal Years 1955 and 1956" (staff paper prepared for the Bureau of the Budget, July 1957), and U.S. Internal Revenue Service, *Bulletin F* (1942).

TABLE F-3. Case II Current Account Surplus or Deficit Adjusted to Reflect the Exclusion of Federal Expenditures for Additions to State, Local and Private Assets, Fiscal Years 1955–63[a]

(In millions of dollars)

Fiscal Year	Change in Current Expenditures		Change in Current Account (3)=(1)−(2)	Case II Current Account Surplus (+) or Deficit (−) (4)	Adjusted Case II Current Account Surplus (+) or Deficit (−) (5)=(3)+(4)
	Added Capital (Lower Current) Expenditures (1)	Added Depreciation Charges (2)			
1955	1,098	545	553	−1,849	−1,296
1956	1,221	594	627	3,409	4,036
1957	543	603	−60	1,489	1,429
1958	790	630	160	−1,555	−1,395
1959	925	664	261	−6,692	−6,431
1960	1,129	699	430	2,588	3,018
1961	1,247	744	503	−2,121	−1,618
1962	1,306	793	513	−4,102	−3,589
1963	1,312	844	468	−3,389	−2,921

[a] Source, Table F-2 and Table 7.

Data obtained from *A Study of Federal Credit Programs*[4] show that the Federal Home Loan Banks (from 1933-1962) and the Federal Land Banks (from 1950-1962) have had no actual losses or losses written off for their credit programs. Thus it was assumed that no estimated loss allowance for these operations was necessary as an adjustment to the Case VII consolidated cash model.

Tables F-3 through F-5 summarize the changes in Models II, V and VII when nonfederally-owned assets are included in the capital account. Each table shows (1) added capital (lower current) expenditures, (2) added depreciation allowances, (3) change in the current account surplus or deficit, (4) the original (Case II, V or VII) current account surplus or deficit, and (5) the new current account surplus or deficit after the capital asset concept has been broadened to include additions to state, local and private assets. In addition to these five items, Table F-5 shows added capital (lower current) receipts as an adjustment to Case VII to arrive at the new current account for the consolidated cash model.

[4] House Subcommittee on Domestic Finance, Committee on Banking and Currency, 88 Cong., 2 sess. (Feb. 28, 1964).

TABLE F-4. Case V Current Account Surplus or Deficit Adjusted to Reflect the Exclusion of Federal Expenditures for Additions to State, Local and Private Assets, Fiscal Years 1955–63[a]

(In millions of dollars)

| Fiscal Year | Change in Current Expenditures | | Change in Current Account (3)=(1)−(2) | Case V Current Account Surplus (+) or Deficit (−) (4) | Adjusted Case V Current Account Surplus (+) or Deficit (−) (5)=(3)+(4) |
	Added Capital (Lower Current) Expenditures (1)	Added Depreciation Charges (2)			
1955	1,098	55	1,043	1,466	2,509
1956	1,221	116	1,105	5,330	6,435
1957	543	143	400	3,148	3,548
1958	790	183	607	−199	408
1959	925	229	696	−5,411	−4,715
1960	1,129	285	844	4,431	5,275
1961	1 247	348	899	−724	175
1962	1,306	413	893	−2,338	−1,445
1963	1,312	479	833	−1,745	−912

[a] Source, Table F-2 and Table 16.

Table F-3 shows the Case II current account surplus or deficit after adjusting for additions to state, local and private assets. Except for 1957 when federal expenditures for nonfederally-owned assets are relatively small, added depreciation allowances are less than the lower current (added capital) expenditures. Although these are admittedly rough estimates, it appears that the difference between the added depreciation allowances and lower current expenditures varies within a range of $400 million and $600 million in most years. In spite of this, however, in no instance does the adjustment for nonfederally-owned assets produce a current account surplus for any year that originally had an administrative budget deficit or a deficit in the original Case II current account. As in the original Case II model, however, the adjusted Case II current account surplus in 1957 is less than the original administrative budget surplus.

Adjusting the Case V current account to exclude federal expenditures for nonfederally-owned assets produces a decidedly different result than it did for the Case II model. As shown in Table F-4, in two years having administrative budget deficits—1958 and 1961—adjusting Case

TABLE F-5. Case VII Current Account Surplus or Deficit Adjusted to Reflect the Exclusion of Federal Expenditures for Additions to State, Local and Private Assets, Fiscal Years 1955–63[a]

(In millions of dollars)

Fiscal year	Change in Current Expenditures		Change in Current Receipts	Change in Current Account $(4)=(1)-[(2)+(3)]$	Case VII Current Account Surplus (+) or Deficit (−) (5)	Adjusted Case VII Current Account Surplus (+) or Deficit (−) $(6)=(4)+(5)$
	Added Capital (Lower Current) Expenditures (1)	Added Depreciation Charges (2)	Added Capital (Lower Current) Receipts (3)			
1955	1,288	545	—	743	−408	335
1956	1,619	594	—	1,025	6,297	7,322
1957	1,605	651	1,479	−525	2,243	1,718
1958	1,757	754	2,028	−1,025	−610	−1,635
1959	4,628	918	2,075	1,635	−7,124	−5,489
1960	4,612	1,106	2,539	967	2,539	3,506
1961	3,728	1,288	2,798	−358	−486	−844
1962	5,083	1,473	2,949	661	−3,016	−2,355
1963	4,788	1,671	3,279	−162	−1,446	−1,608

[a] Source, Table F-2; Table 22; Table E-2.

V produces a current account surplus.[5] In other years, the administrative budget deficits (or surpluses) are considerably lower (higher) as the value of assets excluded from the current account exceeds the additional depreciation allowances, in most years by about $700 million to $1,100 million per year. The fact that the magnitude of these differences is larger than that of differences for the adjusted Case II model reflects the underlying assumption that Case V depreciation allowances are taken only on assets acquired after 1954.

Case VII, one of the consolidated cash budget models, is the final model for which the current account is adjusted to reflect the exclusion of federally-financed but nonfederally-owned assets. The major program expenditures that are excluded from the current account in this model—other than the administrative budget accounts—are the trust fund outlays for the federal highway program and the net expenditures of the Federal Land Banks and the Federal Home Loan Banks. It is not necessary to estimate depreciation or loss allowances for any of these programs since (1) the highway program is financed by earmarked excise taxes which are classified as capital account receipts and (2) the repayment experiences for both of the government-sponsored enterprises do not include any losses over an extended period of time.

As shown in Table F-5, in only one year that had an administrative budget and an original Case VII current account deficit—1955—does an adjusted Case VII current account surplus occur. Over the whole period, the wide variation in the amount of added capital expenditures and added capital receipts is reflected in the widely varying changes in the adjusted Case VII current account surplus or deficit.

---

[5] Of course, in 1955, when there was an administrative budget deficit, the original Case V current account surplus becomes considerably larger after the adjustment for nonfederally-owned assets.

Summary of Budget Surpluses and Deficits

THIS TABLE summarizes administrative and consolidated cash budget surpluses and deficits and compares them with current account surpluses and deficits for each model capital budget. The comparison is made for each fiscal year during the period 1955 to 1963, and for the cumulative total over the whole period.

TABLE G-1. Summary of Current Account Surpluses (+) and Deficits (−), Fiscal Years 1955–63

(In millions of dollars)

Fiscal Year	Administrative Budget	Case I	Case II	Case III	Case IV	Case V	Consolidated Cash Budget	Case VI	Case VII
1955	−4,180	−605	−1,849	3,980	3,895	1,466	−2,702	2,125	−408
1956	1,626	4,700	3,409	7,918	7,573	5,330	4,542	9,208	6,297
1957	1,596	2,965	1,489	6,100	6,443	3,148	2,099	3,847	2,243
1958	−2,819	−227	−1,555	3,518	3,971	−199	−1,580	448	−610
1959	−12,427	−5,464	−6,692	−3,039	−3,206	−5,411	−13,092	−3,342	−7,124
1960	1,224	3,808	2,588	5,413	5,589	4,431	750	5,834	2,539
1961	−3,856	−867	−2,121	146	1,267	−724	−2,300	1,699	−486
1962	−6,378	−2,469	−4,102	−1,975	−159	−2,338	−5,797	753	−3,016
1963	−6,266	−1,911	−3,389	−1,290	991	−1,745	−4,012	1,542	−1,446
Cumulative total	−31,480	−70	−12,222	20,771	26,364	3,958	−22,092	22,114	−2,011

Index

DATE DUE

GAYLORD			PRINTED IN U.S.A.